lonely planet

P9-DGJ-716

POCKET

TOKYO

TOP SIGHTS • LOCAL EXPERIENCES

SIMON RICHMOND, REBECCA MILNER

Contents

Plan Your Trip   4

Tokyo Skytree (p165)
ALEKSANDAR TODOROVIC / SHUTTERSTOCK ©; ARCHITECT: NIKKEN SEKKEI

Explore Tokyo 33

Survival Guide 173

Special Features

COVID-19

We have re-checked every business in this book before publication to ensure that it is still open after the COVID-19 outbreak. However, the economic and social impacts of COVID-19 will continue to be felt long after the outbreak has been contained, and many businesses, services and events referenced in this guide may experience ongoing restrictions. Some businesses may be temporarily closed, have changed their opening hours and services, or require bookings; some unfortunately could have closed permanently. We suggest you check with venues before visiting for the latest information.

Tokyo's Top Experiences

Soak up the atmosphere at Sensō-ji (p156)

Leave the city behind at Meiji-jingū (p102)

Discover the Imperial Palace and Kōkyo-gaien Plaza (p36)

Get arty at teamLab Borderless (p62)

Do it all at Roppongi Hills (p66)

Bar-hop through Golden Gai (p116)

Admire art at Tokyo National Museum (p142)

Take a stroll through Rikugi-en (p152)

Enter the world of Ghibli Museum, Mitaka (p126)

Catch a sumo bout at Ryōgoku Kokugikan (p158)

Plan Your Trip Tokyo's Top Experiences

Enjoy a kabuki show at Kabukiza (p50)

Dining Out

As visitors to Tokyo quickly discover, the people here are absolutely obsessed with food. The city has a vibrant and cosmopolitan dining scene and a strong culture of eating out – popular restaurants are packed most nights of the week. Best of all, you can get superlative meals on any budget.

Tokyo Dining Scene

Tokyo foodies take pride in what they like to think of as their 'boutique' dining scene. Rather than offer long menus of elaborate dishes, many of the best restaurants make just a few things – and sometimes even just one! Sushi shops make sushi; tempura shops make tempura. A restaurant that does too much might be suspect: how can it compare to a speciality shop that has been honing its craft for three generations?

Tokyoites' twin passions for novelty and eating out means that the city is also a hotbed for experimentation. Trends come and go, but one that has stuck around – and spread roots – is the city's home-grown farm-to-table movement. Increasingly, owner-chefs are working directly with rural producers to source ingredients, which might be used in orthodox-style Japanese cooking or creatively, to add a new twist to a classic dish or a fresh take on an imported one.

Izakaya

Izakaya (居酒屋; pictured) translates as 'drinking house' and an evening spent in one is dinner and drinks all in one: food is ordered a few dishes at a time along with rounds of alcoholic drinks. It's fine to order a soft drink instead, but it would be strange to not order at least one drink. Some serve only the classics; others incorporate Western dishes or fusion ones. While the vibe is lively and social, it's perfectly acceptable to go by yourself and sit at the counter.

Best Budget

Commune 2nd Hip outdoor space with vendors serving all kinds of dishes. (p108)

Misojyu Trendy spot for miso soup and creative *onigiri* (rice balls). (p166)

Delifucious Fish burgers from a former sushi chef. (p83)

Best Midrange

Innsyoutei Elegant, but affordable, traditional Japanese in a beautiful wooden building. (p148)

Hantei Skewers of deep-fried meat, fish and vegetables in an old wooden building. (p149)

Best Top End

Kikunoi Tokyo branch of legendary Kyoto *kaiseki* (haute cuisine) restaurant. (p73)

Asakusa Imahan Historic restaurant for top-class sukiyaki (sautéed beef dipped in raw egg). (p167)

Japanese Classics

Kanda Yabu Soba Specialising in soba since 1880. (p136)

Maisen Long-time favourite for *tonkatsu* (deep-friend pork), in a former bathhouse. (p108)

Bird Land Upscale *yakitori* from free-range heirloom chickens. (p58)

Best for Sushi

Kyūbey Rarefied Ginza sushi at its finest. (p58)

Nemuro Hanamaru One of the city's best *kaiten-sushi* (conveyor-belt sushi restaurants). (p44)

Best *Izakaya*

Narukiyo Cult-fave spot on the fringes of Shibuya. (p96)

Shinsuke Century-old local institution adored by sake aficionados. (p150)

Donjaca Vintage mid-20th-century vibe and home-style food. (p121)

Tokyo in a Bowl
Ramen

Broth – the stock is usually made from pork or chicken bones (but sometimes fish bones) and can be flavoured with vegetables, soy sauce or miso.

Noodles – ramen noodles are made from wheat flour mixed with egg and usually *kansui*, an alkaline solution.

Toppings – typical toppings include slices of roast pork *(chāshū)*, bean sprouts, spring onions, thin slices of a *narutomaki* (a fish cake), a boiled egg and sheets of *nori* seaweed.

★ Top Places for Ramen

Nagi (凪; ☏03-3205-1925; www.n-nagi.com; 2nd fl, Golden Gai G2, 1-1-10 Kabukichō, Shinjuku-ku; ramen from ¥890; ◷24hr; ☒ JR Yamanote line to Shinjuku, east exit) Smoky *niboshi* (dried sardine) ramen in late-night haunt, Golden Gai.

Afuri (あふり; www.afuri.com; 1-1-7 Ebisu, Shibuya-ku; ramen from ¥980; ◷11am-5am; ☑; ☒ JR Yamanote line to Ebisu, east exit) Light citrus-y broth and contemporary cool.

Tokyo Rāmen Street (東京ラーメンストリート; Map p40, D3; www.tokyoeki-1bangai.co.jp/ramenstreet; basement, First Avenue, Tokyo Station, 1-9-1 Marunouchi, Chiyoda-ku; ramen from ¥800; ◷7.30am-11.30pm; ☒ JR lines to Tokyo, Yaesu south exit) Eight top vendors clustered at Tokyo station.

Ginza Kazami (銀座風見; ☏03-3572-0737; 6-4-14 Ginza, Chūō-ku; ramen from ¥950; ◷11.30am-3pm & 5.30-10pm Mon-Sat; ⬛ Ginza line to Ginza, exits C2 & C3) Delicious ramen broth flavoured with sake lees.

Noodle Trends

Tokyo has a passion for ramen: the noodles are the subject of profuse blogs and a reason to stand in line for over an hour. By conservative estimates there are over 3000 ramen shops in the capital (some say 4000). One of Tokyo's hottest dining trends is nouveau ramen, creativity distilled in a bowl of noodles and the best budget gourmet experience around. Grabbing late-night ramen after a rousing round of karaoke is a taste sensation you don't want to miss.

LORENANTO / SHUTTERSTOCK ©

Bar Open

Make like Lady Gaga in a karaoke box, sip sake with a merry salaryman in a tiny postwar bar, or dance under the rays of the rising sun at an enormous bayside club: that's nightlife, Tokyo style. The city's drinking culture embraces everything from refined teahouses and indie coffee shops to craft-beer pubs and maid cafes.

Where to Drink

Roppongi has the lion's share of foreigner-friendly bars, while Shinjuku (pictured) offers the retro warren Golden Gai and the LGBTIQ-friendly bar district Ni-chōme.

Other top party districts include youthful Shibuya and Harajuku; Shimbashi and Yūrakuchō, which teem with salarymen; and Ebisu and nearby Daikanyama, both of which have some excellent bars. Asakusa's Hoppy-dōri (p161) is a fun, retro-style hang-out.

What to Drink

Japan's national beverage is sake, aka *nihonshū* (酒 or 日本酒), and is made from rice. According to personal preference, sake can be served hot (*atsukan*) but premium ones are normally served well chilled (*reishu*) in a small jug (*tokkuri*) and poured into tiny cups known as *o-choko* or *sakazuki*.

The clear spirit *shōchū* (焼酎) is made from a variety of raw materials including potato and barley. Because of its potency (alcohol content of around 30%), it is usually served diluted with hot water (*oyu-wari*) or in a *chūhai* cocktail with soft drinks or tea. Sake and *shōchū* are common drinks to order at *izakaya* – along with *nama* (draft beer).

Best Bars

Lonely Classic Golden Gai bar run by the same guy for over 50 years. (p117)

BenFiddich Original cocktails made using freshly ground spices and herbs. (p122)

Gen Yamamoto Savour superior fruit cocktails at this Zen teahouse-like bar. (p74)

Best for Craft Beers

Popeye Get very merry working your way through the most beers on tap in Tokyo. (p168)

Two Dogs Taproom Great range of craft beer and decent pizza in Roppongi. (p74)

Best for Karaoke

Karaoke Rainbow Shibuya's most popular karaoke spot, free for the first hour. (p98)

'Cuzn Homeground Offering a wild night of warbling in Asakusa. (p168)

Pasela Resorts Six floors of rooms in Roppongi. (p74)

Best Clubs

Womb Four levels of lasers and strobes at this Shibuya club fixture. (p98)

Contact Sign up online to get into Tokyo's coolest members-only club. (p97)

Circus Tokyo Underground venue focusing on experimental music. (p96)

Best for Tea

Sakurai Japanese Tea Experience Enjoy a contemporary take on the tea ceremony. (p111)

Cha Ginza Stylish modern version of a teahouse in the heart of Ginza. (p59)

Chashitsu Kaboku A chance to sample super-viscous *koicha* green tea. (p45)

Best for Indie Coffee

Cafe de l'Ambre Ginza institution specialising in aged beans from around the world. (p60)

Iki Espresso Relaxed Aussie-style place serving excellent coffee and breakfasts. (p171)

Treasure Hunt

Since the Edo era, when courtesans set the day's fashions, Tokyoites have lusted after both the novel and the outstanding. The city remains the trendsetter for the nation, and its residents shop – economy be damned – with an infectious enthusiasm. Join them in the hunt for the cutest fashions, the latest gadgets or the perfect teacup.

Where to Shop

Ginza has long been Tokyo's premier shopping district and has many high-end department stores and boutiques, but also fast-fashion emporiums. Harajuku, on the other side of town, has boutiques that deal in both luxury fashion and street cred. Shibuya is the locus of the teen-fashion trend machine.

For one-stop shopping, Shinjuku is ideal: here there are department stores, electronics outfitters, bookshops and more. Asakusa has many stores selling artisan crafts, both traditional and contemporary, which makes it good for souvenir hunting.

Kappabashi-dōri is Tokyo's professional kitchenware district – a great place to source chef's knives and other tools of the Japanese kitchen. So well known for its electronics shops is Akihabara that it is nicknamed 'Denki-gai' – literally 'Electric Town'.

Flea & Antique Markets

Pretty much every weekend there is a flea market happening somewhere, with many taking place at shrines like Shinjuku's Hanazono-jinja (p125), which hosts one every Sunday.

On the first weekend of the month, Raw Tokyo (p110) is a contemporary-style flea market – the kind that has a DJ booth, live painting and food trucks. Quality vendors selling all kinds of vintage items gather for the twice-monthly Ōedo Antique Market (p43).

Duty Free

Department stores, chain stores and,

SEAN K / SHUTTERSTOCK ©; ARCHITECT: KENGO KUMA

increasingly, boutiques offer duty-free shopping. Look for stickers in windows that say 'tax-free shop'. To qualify, you must show your passport and spend more than ¥5000 in any one shop. Otherwise, sales tax is 10%.

Best for Fashion

Kapital Denim woven on vintage looms and lush, hand-dyed textiles. (p85)

House @Mikiri Hassin Hidden spot for under-the-radar local brands. (p112)

Beams Japan Floors of cool Japanese labels, original artwork and contemporary crafts. (p125)

Best for Souvenirs

Tokyu Hands Fascinating emporium of miscellaneous oddities. (p98)

Japan Traditional Crafts Aoyama Square Collection of high-end Japanese artisan work. (p75)

Takumi One-stop shop for earthy traditional crafts from all over Japan. (p61)

Best Malls

Coredo Muromachi Top-class, made-in-Japan fashion and food items. (p47)

Ginza Six High-fashion mall with fantastic art installations. (p60)

KITTE Full of on-trend fashion and homewares boutiques. (pictured; p46)

Best for Design

d47 design travel store Showcase for regional Japanese product design trends and traditions. (p99)

Good Design Store Tokyo by Nohara Goods that have earned Japan's official 'Good Design' stamp of approval. (p47)

Souvenir from Tokyo Curated collection of covetable items from local designers. (p70)

Parks & Gardens

Tokyoites enjoy hectares of open space in the city's many parks – all of which are free to enter. Most of the city's attractive manicured gardens, which cost just a few hundred yen to enter, once belonged to the imperial family or the former feudal elite.

Strolling Gardens

Strolling gardens are meant to be entered and viewed from multiple vantage points along a meandering path, that wends around a central pond. Such gardens have a number of interesting architectural elements, such as bridges, which may be a graceful sloping arch or a simple slab of stone; pavilions, which were created as places for rest or for moon-viewing; or a stone pagoda, often much older than the garden (or even Tokyo!) itself.

Cherry Blossoms

During *hanami* (cherry-blossom viewing), which usually happens in late March or early April, groups of friends and coworkers gather under the *sakura* (cherry blossoms) for sake-drenched picnics. It's a centuries-old tradition, to celebrate the fleeting beauty of life, symbolised by the blossoms that last only a week or two. Ueno-kōen is the classic *hanami* spot. Yoyogi-kōen is where serious party people come armed with barbecues and turntables. Shinjuku-gyoen is a grassy, family-friendly location for lazing under the blossoms.

Autumn Leaves

The city's trees undergo magnificent seasonal transformations during *kōyō* (autumn foliage season), which usually hits Tokyo in late November and early December. Koishikawa Kōrakuen and Hama-rikyū Onshi-teien are known for their spectacular displays.

NADEZDA ZAVITAEVA / SHUTTERSTOCK ©

Best Gardens

Rikugi-en Tokyo's most beautiful strolling garden, evoking scenes from classical literature. (p152)

Hama-rikyū Onshi-teien An ancient shogunate hunting ground, now a vast green space with a traditional teahouse. (pictured; p55)

Kiyosumi-teien A former villa pleasure garden with sculptural stones from around Japan. (p171)

Koishikawa Kōrakuen A classic example of traditional Japanese garden design, in the middle of the city. (p135)

Best Parks

Ueno-kōen Tokyo's oldest park with museums, temples, woodsy paths and water lilies. (p148)

Shinjuku-gyoen Home to 1500 cherry trees, vast lawns and a tropical greenhouse. (p119)

Yoyogi-kōen A big grassy expanse and a popular weekend gathering spot. (p107)

Inokashira-kōen Wooded strolling paths, performance artists and pedal boats. (p127)

Best Hanami-Viewing

Ueno-kōen Cherry trees burst into blossom in spring, making this one of Tokyo's top *hanami* spots. (p148)

Meguro-gawa Lined with cherry trees and a walking path, the Meguro-gawa (not so much a river as a canal) is a great spot for a hot wine under the blossoms. (p79)

Shinjuku-gyoen Don't miss the greenhouse; the Taiwanese-style pavilion (Goryō-tei) that overlooks the garden's central pond; and the cherry blossoms in spring. (p119)

Architecture

Little traditional wooden architecture has survived into 21st-century Tokyo. However, what is abundant here are striking and imaginative works by the country's contemporary architects, riffing on old designs and contemplating the new. It's easy to see why they are among the most influential and acclaimed architects in the world.

WORLDPICTURES / SHUTTERSTOCK ©

Notable Architects

The most influential architect of the 1960s was Tange Kenzō (1913–2005) – his landmark structures include the National Gymnasium (1964) in Yoyogi-kōen and St Mary's Cathedral, Tokyo (1955). Among his contemporaries were the Metabolists Kurokawa Kishō and Maki Fumihiko, whose design philosophy championed flexible spaces over fixed form.

Of the current generation Tadao Ando and Ito Toyo are stars. Ando's works in modern materials such as concrete and steel while Ito's designs are lighter and more conceptual.

Kengo Kuma has been the go-to architect for high-profile commissions across Tokyo over the last decade: he's behind the National Stadium for the 2021 Tokyo Summer Olympics.

Best Architecture

Tokyo Metropolitan Government Building Gotham-like complex by Tange Kenzō with twin observatories. (p119)

21_21 Design Sight Ando-designed museum devoted to contemporary design. (p70)

Nakagin Capsule Tower High-concept landmark by Kurokawa Kishō from the 1960s. (p56)

Tokyo International Forum Soaring glass vessel designed by Rafael Viñoly. (pictured; p43)

Nezu Museum Kengo Kuma designed this museum's striking building. (p107)

Pop Culture

From giant robots to a certain ubiquitous kitty, Japanese pop culture is a massive phenomenon that has reached far around the world. At the centre of the manga (Japanese comics) and anime (Japanese animation) vortex is the neighbourhood of Akihabara. For eye-popping street fashion, look to Shibuya and Harajuku.

SHIN GODZILLA: TOHO CO., LTD.
OSUGI / SHUTTERSTOCK ©

Tokyo's Pop Culture Districts

Akihabara is the centre of any pop-culture Tokyo tour. With its multitude of stores selling anime- and manga-related goods, not to mention maid cafes and all the electronic gizmos imaginable, Akiba (as it's known to locals) is peak geek territory.

Harajuku remains the best place to survey Tokyo's street style. More wannabe street fashionistas strut their stuff a little further south in Tokyo's trend-mecca,

Shibuya. The artificial island of Odaiba with its outlandish architecture and zippy monorail feels like an anime version of Tokyo.

Northwestern Tokyo districts of Takadanobaba and Ikebukuro are also home to a cluster of anime- and manga-related sites and shops, as are the western Tokyo suburbs of Mitaka, Nakano and Suginami.

Best Pop Culture Experiences

Ghibli Museum, Mitaka
Enter the magical world of

famed animator Miyazaki Hayao. (p126)

Godzilla Don't miss your chance to take a photo with Godzilla, the famous monster of Japanese cinema. (pictured; p56)

Ni-Tele Really Big Clock Animated timepiece designed in collaboration with Miyazaki in the middle of downtown. (p56)

Robot Restaurant See Shinjuku's wacky cabaret costarring giant robots. (p122)

Kawaii Monster Cafe Check out the surreal installations and fashions. (p108)

Museums & Galleries

Tokyo has many excellent museums, including both grand repositories of art and antiquities and tiny centres of devotion to one particular thing. The city is the centre of Japan's contemporary art scene; though it doesn't have a cohesive arts district, many galleries are clustered in Ginza or around Roppongi.

F11PHOTO / SHUTTERSTOCK ©

Access & Admission

Many museums close on Mondays (or, if Monday is a national holiday, then the following Tuesday). Museums tend to close early, around 5pm or 6pm, and last admission is 30 minutes before closing. Take advantage of the free lockers (¥100 deposit) to stow your coat and bag. Permanent exhibits at national museums are the most economical; expect to pay more for admission to temporary exhibits or private museums. Concessions are often available for students and seniors; bring ID. Commercial galleries are free to enter.

Best Museums

Tokyo National Museum Home to the world's largest collection of Japanese art. (pictured; p142)

Nezu Museum Asian antiques in a striking contemporary building. (p107)

Mori Art Museum Contemporary shows by top Japanese and foreign artists. (p67)

TOP Museum The city's photography museum. (p81)

Japan Folk Crafts Museum Exhibitions of artisan craftwork. (p92)

Intermediatheque Experimental museum drawing on the holdings of the University of Tokyo. (p41)

Best Galleries

Okuno Building Vintage Ginza apartment block crammed with tiny galleries. (p53)

Complex 665 Houses three leading commercial art galleries. (p71)

SCAI the Bathhouse Cutting-edge contemporary art in a renovated bathhouse. (p145)

Temples & Shrines

Tokyo's many Buddhist temples and Shintō shrines honour Japan's two entwined religions. These rare-in-Tokyo examples of traditional architecture often look quite similar; shrines can be identified by their distinctive torii gates, composed of two upright pillars, joined at the top by two horizontal crossbars.

COWARDLION / SHUTTERSTOCK ©

Visiting Etiquette

Shrines and temples don't have strict rules (there are no dress codes, for example); however, there are some prescribed manners.

The grounds are free to enter and open to all, so long as the gate is open. Since the *torii* indicates the entrance to sacred space, you'll often see Japanese visitors bowing upon entering and exiting. As Shintō prizes purity, shrines also have fonts where visitors wash their hands before approaching the main hall.

Temples often have a slightly raised threshold, which you should step over – not on. Taking pictures on the grounds is fine, but many temples do not want you taking photos – especially flash photos – of the inside. It's also respectful to keep your voice down.

Best Temples

Sensō-ji The city's oldest and most famous Buddhist temple, and the epicentre of old-world Asakusa. (p156)

Zōjō-ji The official funerary temple for the Tokugawa shogunate, with a rare 17th-century gate and bell. (p71)

Best Shrines

Meiji-jingū Tokyo's grandest Shintō shrine, set in a wooded grove. (p102)

Ueno Tōshō-gū Gilded homage to the warlord who put Tokyo on the map, Tokugawa Ieyasu. (p148)

Kanda Myōjin Important shrine with a special connection to nearby Akihabara. (p135)

Nezu-jinja Pretty shrine with a photogenic stretch of red *torii* gates. (pictured; p147)

For Kids

Tokyo is a parent's dream: hyperclean, safe and with every mod con. While most of the top attractions aren't that appealing to little ones, older kids and teens should get a kick out of Tokyo's pop culture. Shibuya and Harajuku in particular are packed with the shops, restaurants and arcades that local teens love.

KUREMO / SHUTTERSTOCK ©

Travelling with Children

In central Tokyo (where few families live) large chains (such as Jonathan's, Royal Host and Gusto) are the most family-friendly eating options: they have large booths, high chairs, nonsmoking sections and children's menus (usually with Western food). Most hotels have cots for a small fee, but it's near impossible to find a room with two double beds (that isn't an expensive suite). Ryokan usually have rooms that can accommodate four or five people on futons.

Best Family Fun

Ghibli Museum, Mitaka A portal to the magical world of famed animator Miyazaki Hayao (*Ponyo*, *Spirited Away*). (p126)

Tokyo Dome City Thrill rides (plus more sedate rides for little ones) and a Ferris wheel with karaoke-equipped gondolas. (pictured; p138)

Sakurazaka-kōen Neighbourhood park with robot-themed play equipment. (p67)

Best Activities

Mokuhankan Learn the Japanese art of making woodblock prints here. (p166)

Toyokuni Atelier Gallery Get a taster of *sumie*, the art of ink painting on *washi* (Japanese paper). (p135)

Best Museums

teamLab Borderless Kids can interact with digital artworks and even create their own. (p62)

TeNQ Part of Tokyo Dome City, this interactive museum is all about outer space. (p135)

LGBTIQ+

Tokyo is generally a LGBTIQ+ tolerant city and has made great strides in the past couple of years towards openness and acceptance; still, many LGBTIQ+ people remain fearful of living publicly out – outside of safe spaces like Shinjuku-nichōme ('Nichōme' for short), the city's largest and liveliest gay quarter.

PATARA / SHUTTERSTOCK ©

Law & Attitudes

There are no legal restraints on same-sex sexual activities in Japan, apart from the usual age restrictions. Outright discrimination is unusual; however, travellers have reported being turned away or grossly overcharged when checking into love hotels with a partner of the same sex. Such discrimination is illegal, but is rarely litigated. One thing to keep in mind: Japanese people, regardless of their sexual orientation, do not typically engage in public displays of affection.

What's Going On

To keep up to date with issues concerning Tokyo's LGBTIQ+ community, and to learn about events and meet-ups, follow the **Nichōme Community Project** (@NichomeComProj) and **Nijiro News** (@nijinews) on twitter. **Utopia Asia** (www. utopia-asia.com) has lots of resources and recommendations for LGBTIQ+ travellers.

Best LGBTIQ+ Venues

Eagle Pose in front of manga artist Inuyoshi's great mural of beefy guys. (p122)

Aiiro Cafe Start your Ni-chōme night at this popular corner bar. (p124)

Bar Goldfinger Friendly vibe at this lesbian bar designed to look like a '70s motel. (p124)

Arty Farty Rub shoulders (and other body parts) on this bar's packed dance floor. (p124)

Four Perfect Days

Day 1

SEAN PAVONE / SHUTTERSTOCK ©

Visit **Meiji-jingū** (p102), Tokyo's signature Shintō shrine. Walk down stylish **Omote-sandō** (p104), lined with stunning contemporary architecture, and drop by the **Ukiyo-e Ōta Memorial Museum of Art** (p107).

Lunch at **Maisen** (p108) then walk to Tokyo's most photogenic (and chaotic) intersection, **Shibuya Crossing** (pictured; p93). Follow **Shibuya Centergai** (p93) to find supreme souvenir hunting ground **Tokyu Hands** (p98).

Take the train to Shinjuku and grab an early dinner in **Omoideyokochō** (p120). The **Tokyo Metropolitan Government Building** (p119) observatories stay open until 11pm for free night views. Enjoy late-night drinks in **Golden Gai** (p116).

Day 2

FOOD FOTO PHOTOGRAPHY / GETTY IMAGES ©

Breakfast on take-away food at **Tsukiji Market** (pictured; p55). There are also stalls selling kitchen tools, tea and more. Walk to the landscaped garden **Hama-rikyū Onshi-teien** (p55), where you can enjoy the view sipping tea at **Nakajima no Ochaya** (p55).

Enjoy an indulgent sushi lunch at **Kyūbey** (p58; reservations necessary), then explore Ginza's art galleries and luxury boutiques. Hop on the overground Yurikamome line to Odaiba, home to the fascinating digital-art museum, **teamLab Borderless** (p62).

Return to the city centre for dinner at **Nihonbashi Tamai** (p45) and to see traditional performing arts at dinner theatre **Suigian** (p45).

Day 3

TAKASHI IMAGES / SHUTTERSTOCK ©

Hit Tokyo's top temple **Sensō-ji** (pictured; p156) early, then explore Asakusa's maze of narrow lanes packed with shops selling traditional crafts and foodstuffs.

Spend the afternoon exploring the many attractions of **Ueno-kōen** (p141), including **Tokyo National Museum** (p142) and centuries-old temples and shrines. Continue on to the charming historical neighbourhood of Yanaka, zoning in on the traditional shopping street **Yanaka Ginza** (p145).

Back in Ueno, stroll through the old-fashioned market, **Ameya-yokochō** (p151). Dine at iconic *izakaya* (Japanese pub-eatery) **Shinsuke** (p150), then return to Asakusa to see Sensō-ji lit up (and deserted) and catch a folk-music show at **Oiwake** (p168).

Day 4

Reserve a 10am slot to visit the magical **Ghibli Museum, Mitaka** (p126). Afterwards walk through **Inokashira-kōen** (pictured; p127), and either have lunch or a picnic there.

Take the Chūō line back east to geek-fest Akihabara, where you can ride go-karts with **MariCAR** (p137) and buy quality craft souvenirs from **2k540 Aki-Oka Artisan** (p138).

Clean up afterwards with an onsen dip at nearby **Spa La-Qua** (p139), followed by dinner at **Kado** (p137) in Kagurazaka. Head to **Roppongi Hills** (p66), home to the excellent **Mori Art Museum** (p67), which stays open until 10pm. After, dive into Roppongi's infamous nightlife. Make sure to get in a round of karaoke.

Need to Know

For detailed information, see Survival Guide p173

Currency
Japanese yen (¥)

Language
Japanese

Visas
Visas are generally not required for stays of up to 90 days.

Money
Convenience stores and post offices have international ATMs. Credit cards are widely accepted, but keep some cash on hand.

Mobile Phones
Prepaid data-only SIM cards (for unlocked smartphones only) are available at the airport or electronics stores. Many hotels now offer Handy phone service.

Time
Japan Standard Time (GMT/UTC plus nine hours)

Tipping
Tipping is not common practice in Japan. Top-end restaurants will add a 10% service charge.

Daily Budget

Budget: Less than ¥8000

Dorm bed: ¥3000

Free sights such as temples and markets

Bowl of noodles: ¥800

Happy-hour drink: ¥500

24-hour subway pass: ¥600

Midrange: ¥8000–20,000

Double room at a business hotel: ¥15,000

Museum entry: ¥1000

Dinner for two at an *izakaya*: ¥6000

Live music show: ¥3000

Top End: More than ¥20,000

Double room in a four-star hotel: from ¥35,000

Private cooking class: ¥10,000

Sushi-tasting menu: ¥15,000

Taxi ride back to the hotel: ¥3000

Advance Planning

Three months before Purchase tickets for Ghibli Museum, Mitaka (p126); book a table at a top restaurant.

One month before Book tickets online for theatre and sporting events, activities, courses and tours of the Imperial Palace (p36).

When you arrive Look for discount coupons for attractions at airports and hotels; have your accommodation help you reserve seats at popular *izakaya* (Japanese pub-eateries).

Arriving in Tokyo

✈ From Narita Airport

An express train or highway bus to central Tokyo costs around ¥3000 (one to two hours). Both run frequently from 6am to 10.30pm; pick up tickets at kiosks inside the arrivals hall (no advance reservations required). Taxis start at ¥20,000.

✈ From Haneda Airport

Frequent trains and buses (¥400 to ¥1200, 30 to 45 minutes) to central Tokyo run frequently from 5.30am to midnight; times and costs depend on your destination in the city. There are only a couple of night buses. For a taxi, budget between ¥5000 and ¥8000.

🚃 From Tokyo Station

Connect from the shinkansen (bullet train) terminal at Tokyo Station (pictured) to the JR Yamanote line or the Marunouchi subway to destinations around central Tokyo.

Getting Around

Efficient, clean and generally safe, Tokyo's public transport system is the envy of the world. Of most use to travellers is the train and subway system, which is easy to navigate thanks to English signage.

S Subway

The quickest and easiest way to get around central Tokyo. Runs 5am to midnight.

🚃 Train

Japan Rail (JR) Yamanote (loop) and Chūō-Sōbu (central) lines service major stations. Runs from 5am to midnight.

🚕 Taxi

A pricey option but the only one that runs all night; easy to hail.

🚲 Cycling

Fun, but traffic can be intense. Rentals available; some hostels and ryokan lend bicycles.

🚶 Walking

Subway stations are close in the city centre; and walkable if you're only going one stop.

Tokyo Neighbourhoods

Shinjuku (p115)
Tokyo's biggest hub has the world's busiest train station, the city hall, a sprawling park, shopping and nightlife.

Kagurazaka, Kōrakuen & Around (p129)
An atmospheric hill with old-world alleys and hidden restaurants, a traditional garden, Tokyo's top baseball stadium and the geek heaven of Akihabara.

◉ *Rikugi-en*

Harajuku & Aoyama (p101)
Home to Tokyo's grandest Shintō shrine, this nexus of tradition and trends swarms with shoppers and luxury-brand architecture.

◉ *Golden Gai*

◉ *Meiji-jingū*

Imperial Palace ◉

◉ *Roppongi Hills*

Shibuya (p87)
The centre of Tokyo's youth culture looks like the set of a sci-fi flick, with a collection of giant TV screens, lurid fashion and crowds.

Ebisu, Meguro & Around (p77)
A collection of funky neighbourhoods, with stylish boutiques, unexpected museums, and excellent restaurants and bars.

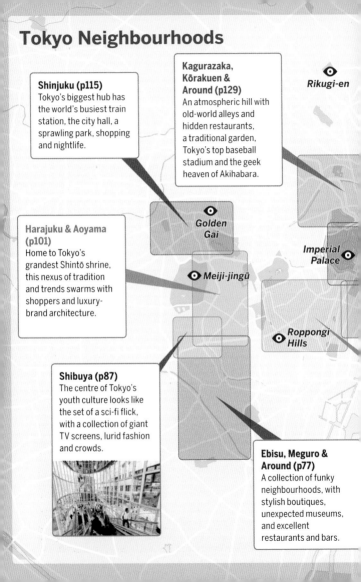

Tokyo National Museum

Ueno & Yanesen (p141)
Tokyo's most famous museum, plus temples, shrines and residential neighbourhoods where time seems to have stopped decades ago.

Sensō-ji

Ryōgoku Kokugikan

Asakusa, Ryōgoku & Sumida River (p155)
The traditional heart of Tokyo, a riverside district of ancient temples, old merchants' quarters, and nostalgic restaurants and bars.

Marunouchi & Nihombashi (p35)
History meets modernity when the grounds of the Imperial Palace meet the skyscrapers of Marunouchi.

Kabukiza

Ginza (p49)
Tokyo's classiest neighbourhood, with department stores, boutiques, gardens, teahouses and high-end restaurants.

teamLab Borderless

Roppongi, Akasaka & Around (p65)
Legendary for its nightlife, this forward-looking neighbourhood is also the place for cutting-edge art, architecture and design.

Explore
Tokyo

Worth a Trip 🔭

Tokyo's Walking Tours 🥾

Shinjuku (p115) MR. JAMES KELLEY / SHUTTERSTOCK ©

Marunouchi & Nihombashi

The Imperial Palace is Tokyo's geographic centre, a sprawling green space that includes the now public park, Kitanomaru-kōen, home to museums. Nearby Marunouchi is a high-powered business district; it's Tokyo's establishment at its finest, with glossy skyscrapers and monumental architecture, but also restaurants, bars and shops for the office workers who hold it all together.

The Short List

○ **Imperial Palace (p36)** *Stroll through the manicured gardens surrounding the emperor's home.*

○ **Intermediatheque (p41)** *View the amazing, eclectic collection of Tokyo University.*

○ **Tokyo International Forum (p43)** *Gaze up at the vast atrium of this convention and arts centre.*

○ **National Museum of Modern Art (MOMAT; p39)** *See impressive works by both Japanese and international artists.*

○ **Nihombashi (p42)** *Eyeball the sculpted dragons on Tokyo's most famous bridge.*

Getting There & Around

🚆 Many services stop at Tokyo Station. Yūrakuchō Station is also convenient for the area.

Ⓢ The Marunouchi line connects with Tokyo Station. The Mita, Chiyoda and Hanzōmon lines also have stops nearby. The Ginza line is handy for Nihombashi.

Neighbourhood Map on p40

Top Experience 📷

Discover the Imperial Palace & Kōkyo-gaien Plaza

Japan's Imperial Palace (皇居, Kōkyo) occupies the site of the original Edo-jō, the castle of the Tokugawa shogunate (who ruled from 1603 to 1868). In its heyday this was the largest fortress in the world, though little remains of it today apart from the moat and stone walls. The present palace (Kyūden) is home to the Japanese imperial family.

◎ MAP P40, B3

📞 03-5223-8071

http://sankan.kunaicho.go.jp

1 Chiyoda, Chiyoda-ku

admission free

🕐 tours usually 10am & 1.30pm Tue-Sat

Ⓢ Chiyoda line to Ōtemachi, exits C13b & C10

Palace Tours

Most of the palace grounds are off limits. If you wish to see a small part of the palace's inner compound you'll need to join an official tour organised by the Imperial Household Agency. Reservations are taken – via the website, phone or by post – up to a month in advance. Alternatively, go to the office at **Kikyō-mon** (桔梗門; 1 Chiyoda, Chiyoda-ku; ⏰tour bookings 8.45am-noon & 1-5pm); if there is space available on the tour, you'll be able to register.

Imperial Palace East Garden

Crafted from part of the original castle compound, the **Imperial Palace East Garden** (東御苑, Kōkyo Higashi-gyoen; http://sankan.kunaicho.go.jp; 1 Chiyoda, Chiyoda-ku; admission free; ⏰9am-4pm Nov-Feb, to 4.30pm Mar–mid-Apr, Sep & Oct, to 5pm mid-Apr–Aug, closed Mon & Fri year-round) allows you to get up-close views of the massive stones used to build the castle walls, and even climb the ruins of the main keep, off the upper lawn. The large lawn is where the Honmaru (central part of the castle) was once located. Entry is free, but the number of visitors at any one time is limited, so it never feels crowded. There are three gates: most people enter through **Ōte-mon** (大手門), the closest gate to Tokyo Station, and once the principal entrance to Edo-jō.

Kōkyo-gaien Plaza

This grassy **expanse** (皇居外苑広場, Kōkyo-gaien Hiroba; www.env.go.jp/garden/kokyogaien; 1 Chiyoda, Chiyoda-ku; Ⓢ Hibiya line to Hibiya, exit B6) southeast of the palace compound is planted with roughly 2000 immaculately maintained Japanese black pine trees. From the plaza you can see the iron **Nijū-bashi** and the stone **Megane-bashi** within the palace compound.

★ **Top Tips**

○ Tours (lasting around 1¼ hours) usually run at 10am and 1.30pm Tuesday to Saturday, but not on public holidays or afternoons from late July through to the end of August; check the website for the complete schedule.

○ Two-hour guided walking tours of the Imperial Palace East Garden are led in English by volunteer members of the Tokyo Systematized Goodwill Guide (SGG) Club; meet at the JNTO Tourist Information Center (p181) before 1pm.

✕ **Take a Break**

Wind down the day with a cocktail at **Peter: the Bar** (☎03-6270-2763; http://tokyo.peninsula.com/en/fine-dining/peter-lounge-bar; 24th fl, 1-8-1 Yūrakuchō, Chiyoda-ku; ⏰noon-midnight, to 1am Fri & Sat; Ⓢ Hibiya line to Hibiya, exits A6 & A7), which is adjacent to Kōkyo-gaien Plaza.

Walking Tour 🥾

Strolling the Imperial Palace Grounds

This walk starts in woodsy Kitanomaru-kōen, the northern part of the Imperial Palace's compound and home to several excellent museums. It continues into the Imperial Palace East Garden and towards Tokyo Station.

Walk Facts

Start Nippon Budōkan; Ⓢ Kudanshita Station, exit 2

End Wadakura Fountain Park; 🚉 Tokyo Station

Length 1.5km; two to three hours

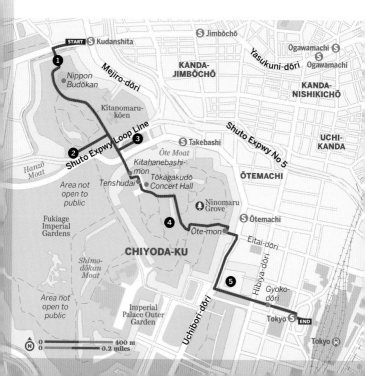

❶ Nippon Budōkan

Walk uphill and across the Ushiga-fuchi moat to Tayasu-mon. The northern gate to Kitanomaru-kōen was once part of the castle Edo-jō. Just inside the park is the **Nippon Budōkan** (日本武道館; ☎ 03-3216-5100; www.nipponbudokan.or.jp; 2-3 Kitanomaru-kōen, Chiyoda-ku), a concert and martial-arts hall originally built for the 1964 Olympics; it was pressed into service again for the 2021 event.

❷ Crafts Gallery

Follow the road south, branching off to the right to find the **Crafts Gallery** (東京国立近代美術館 工芸館; www.momat.go.jp; 1 Kitanomaru-kōen, Chiyoda-ku; adult/child ¥250/free, 1st Sun of month free; ⊙10am-5pm Tue-Sun), a handsome recreation of a red-brick building that was once the headquarters of the imperial guards.

❸ MOMAT

View some exceptional artworks at the **National Museum of Modern Art (MOMAT)** (国立近代美術館, Kokuritsu Kindai Bijutsukan; ☎ 03-5777-8600; www.momat.go.jp; 3-1 Kitanomaru-kōen, Chiyoda-ku; adult/child ¥500/free, 1st Sun of month free; ⊙10am-5pm Tue-Thu & Sun, to 8pm Fri & Sat); on the 4th floor, the 'Room with a View' provides a beautiful multilayered panorama of your next destination: the Imperial Palace East Garden, with the towers of Ōtemachi and Marunouchi in the background.

❹ Imperial Palace East Garden

Cross the Ōte Moat and enter the palace gardens via Kitahanebashi-mon. Beyond the gate is **Tenshu-dai**, all that remains of the castle's main keep. Climb the stone base for views across the lawn towards the octagonal **Tōkagakudō Concert Hall**, which has a petal-shaped roof and outer scalloped walls covered with delicate murals made from ceramics and pottery shards. Move on to the Ninomaru Grove, a woodland area that is one of the prettiest parts of the garden with a pond and the elegant Suwano-chaya teahouse. Exit the gardens via the Ōte-mon, the old main gate to the castle.

❺ Wadakura Fountain Park

Across the road is **Wadakura Fountain Park** (和田倉噴水公園; www.env.go.jp/garden/kokyogaien/english/point04.html; 1-3 Kōkyo-gaien, Chiyoda-ku; admission free; S Chiyoda line to Ōtemachi, exits C13b & C10); the two fountains here celebrate the weddings of the current and past emperor and empress. Next to the park is the pedestrianised central reservation of ginko-tree-lined Gyoko-dōri. It provides the perfect frame from which to admire the elegant brick facade and twin domes of Tokyo Station.

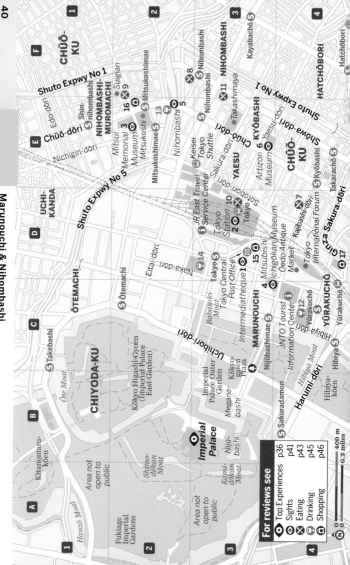

Marunouchi & Nihombashi

CHŪŌ-KU

Shuto Expwy No 1

Edo-dōri

Chūō-dōri

Nichigin-dōri

Suigian ● 9 ⊗
16 ⊗ Shin-
Shin- nihombashi Ⓢ
nihombashi Ⓢ
NIHOMBASHI-
MUROMACHI 13 Mitsukoshimae Ⓢ
3 Mitsui 5 ⊗
Memorial ⊗ Mitsukoshi
Museum Mitsukoshimae Ⓢ
Nihombashi Ⓢ

⊗ 8
Ⓢ Nihombashi
NIHOMBASHI

⊗ 11
Takashimaya

Kayabachō Ⓢ

HATCHŌBORI

Hatchōbori Ⓢ

Shuto Expwy No 1

Showa-dōri

Yaesu-dōri

KYŌBASHI

CHŪŌ-
KU

Kyōbashi Ⓢ

Takarachō Ⓢ

Shuto Expwy No 5

UCHI-
KANDA

Takebashi Ⓢ

Ōtemachi Ⓢ

ŌTEMACHI

CHIYODA-KU

Ōte Moat

Kitanomaru-
kōen

Hanzō Moat

Shimo-
dōkan Moat

Fukiage
Imperial Gardens

Kōkyo Higashi-Gyoen
(Imperial Palace
East Garden)

Imperial
Palace Outer
Garden

Kōkyo-
gaien Plaza

Megane-
bashi

Area not
open to
public

Kami-
dōkan Moat

Area not
open to
public

◉ Imperial
Palace

Nijū-
bashi

Sakuradamon Ⓢ

Keisei
Tokyo
Shuttle

Mitsukoshimae Ⓢ

JR East Travel
Service Center ⊕

Tokyo
Station 10 ⊕
2 Ⓚ
Tokyo Ⓢ

Artizon 6
Museum

YAESU

Sotobori-dōri

Sakura-dōri

Chūō-dōri

Eitai-dōri

Naka-dōri

⊕ 14

Tokyo Ⓢ
Tokyo Central
Post Office

Babasaki
Moat

Intermediatheque ⊕

Uchibori-dōri

MARUNOUCHI

Nijūbashimae Ⓢ

JNTO Tourist
Information Center ⊕

Hibiya-dōri

Hibiya Moat

Hibiya-
kōen

Harumi-dōri

4 Mitsubishi
Ichigōkan Museum ⊕

15 ⊕

Ōedo Antique
Market

Tokyo
International Forum

Kajibashi-dōri

Ginza-itchōme Ⓢ

Ginza Sakura-dōri

⊗ 7

⊗ 17

HIBIYA

YŪRAKUCHŌ

Yūrakuchō Ⓢ

12 ⊕

Yūrakuchō Ⓢ

Hibiya Ⓢ

For reviews see

◉	Top Experiences	p36
◉	Sights	p41
⊗	Eating	p43
⊕	Drinking	p45
⊕	Shopping	p46

0 ⎯⎯⎯ 400 m
0 ⎯⎯⎯ 0.2 miles

Sights

Intermediatheque
MUSEUM

1 ◎ MAP P40, D3

Dedicated to interdisciplinary experimentation, Intermediatheque cherry-picks from the vast collection of the University of Tokyo (Tōdai) to craft a fascinating, contemporary museum experience. Go from viewing the best ornithological taxidermy collection in Japan to a giant pop-art print or the beautifully encased skeleton of a dinosaur. A handsome Tōdai lecture hall is reconstituted as a forum for events, including the playing of 1920s jazz recordings on a gramophone or old movie screenings. (インターメ ディアテク; ☎03-5777-8600; www. intermediatheque.jp; 2nd & 3rd fl, JP Tower, 2-7-2 Marunouchi, Chiyoda-ku; admission free; ⏰11am-6pm, to 8pm Fri & Sat, usually closed Sun & Mon; ☒JR Yamanote line to Tokyo, Marunouchi exit)

Tokyo Station
LANDMARK

2 ◎ MAP P40, D3

Tokyo Station celebrated its centenary in 2014 with a major renovation and expansion. Tatsuno Kingo's original elegant brick building on the Marunouchi side has been expertly restored to include domes faithful to the original design, decorated inside with relief sculptures. It's best viewed straight on from the plaza on Miyuki-dōri.

(東京駅; www.tokyostationcity.com; 1-9 Marunouchi, Chiyoda-ku; ☒JR lines to Tokyo Station)

Mitsui Memorial Museum
MUSEUM

3 ◎ MAP P40, E2

Stately wood panelling surrounds a small collection of traditional Japanese art and artefacts, including ceramics, paintings and *nō* (stylised dance-drama) masks, amassed over three centuries by the families behind today's Mitsui conglomerate. (三井記 念美術館; ☎03-5777-8600; www. mitsui-museum.jp; 7th fl, Mitsui Main Bldg, 2-1-1 Nihombashi-Muromachi, Chūō-ku; adult/student ¥1000/500; ⏰10am-5pm Tue-Sun; ⑤Ginza line to Mitsukoshimae, exit A7)

Mitsubishi Ichigōkan Museum
MUSEUM

4 ◎ MAP P40, C3

Housed in a handsome reproduction of the area's first office building (designed in 1894 by English architect Josiah Conder), this museum showcases European art from the late 19th to the mid-20th centuries, with a focus on its holdings of Toulouse-Lautrec works. (三菱一号館美術 館; ☎03-5777-8600; http://mimt.jp; 2-6-2 Marunouchi, Chiyoda-ku; admission varies by exhibition; ⏰10am-6pm Tue-Thu, Sat & Sun, to 9pm Fri & 2nd Wed of month; ⑤Chiyoda line to Nijūbashimae, exit 1)

Nihombashi

Nihombashi BRIDGE

5 ⦿ MAP P40, E2

Guarded by bronze lions and dragons, this handsome 1911-vintage granite bridge over the Nihonbashi-gawa is partly obscured by the overhead expressway. During the Edo period this was the beginning of the great trunk roads (the Tōkaidō, the Nikkō Kaidō etc) that took *daimyō* (domain lords) between the capital and their home provinces. It's still the point from which distances to Tokyo are measured. (日本橋, Nihonbashi; 1 Nihombashi, Chūō-ku; Ⓢ Ginza line to Mitsukoshimae, exits B5 & B6)

Artizon Museum MUSEUM

6 ⦿ MAP P40, E3

Amassed by Bridgestone founder Ishibashi Shōjiro, this is one of the best French impressionist collections you will find in Asia. The European paintings are undoubtedly the main attraction (think Renoir, Ingres, Monet, Corot, Matisse, Picasso, Kandinsky et al). (☎03-3563-0241; www.bridgestone-museum.gr.jp; 1-10-1 Kyōbashi, Chūō-ku; adult/student ¥800/500; ⊙10am-6pm Tue-Thu, Sat & Sun, to 8pm Fri; Ⓢ Ginza line to Kyōbashi, exit 6)

Tokyo International Forum

An architectural marvel designed by Rafael Viñoly, **Tokyo International Forum** (東京国際フォーラム; Map p40, D4; ☏03-5221-9000; www.t-i-forum.co.jp; 3-5-1 Marunouchi, Chiyoda-ku; admission free; ⏱7am-11.30pm; 🚃JR Yamanote line to Yūrakuchō, central exit) houses a convention and arts centre, with eight auditoriums and a spacious courtyard in which concerts and events are held. The eastern wing looks like a glass ship plying the urban waters; you can access the catwalks from the 7th floor (take the lift).

Held here usually on the first and third Sunday of every month (check the website before you head out), **Ōedo Antique Market** (大江戸骨董市; Map p40, D4; ☏03-6407-6011; www.antique-market.jp; ⏱9am-4pm 1st & 3rd Sun of month; 🚃JR Yamanote line to Yūrakuchō, Kokusai Forum exit) is a brilliantly colourful event with hundreds of dealers in retro and antique Japanese goods, from old ceramics and kimonos to kitsch plastic figurines and vintage movie posters.

Eating

Dhaba India

SOUTH INDIAN ¥

7 ✕ MAP P40, D4

Indian meals in Tokyo don't come much better than those served at this long-established restaurant with deep-indigo plaster walls. The food is very authentic, particularly the curries served with basmati rice, naan or crispy *dosa* (giant lentil-flour pancakes). Set lunches are spectacularly good value. (ダバ インディア; ☏03-3272-7160; www.dhabaindia.com; 2-7-9 Yaesu, Chūō-ku; lunch/mains from ¥850/1370; ⏱11.15am-3pm & 5-11pm Mon-Fri, noon-3pm & 5-10pm Sat & Sun; 🚇Ginza line to Kyōbashi, exit 5)

Taimeiken

JAPANESE ¥

8 ✕ MAP P40, F2

This classic restaurant, open since 1931, specialises in *yōshoku* – Western cuisine adapted to the Japanese palate. Its signature dish is *omuraisu* (an omelette stuffed with ketchup-flavoured fried rice), to which you can add a side of borscht and coleslaw for the very retro price of ¥50 each. The *tampopo omuraisu* was created for Itami Jūzō's cult movie. (たいめいけん; ☏03-3271-2463; www.taimeiken.co.jp; 1-12-10 Nihombashi, Chūō-ku; mains ¥750-2650; ⏱11am-8.30pm Mon-Sat, to 8pm Sun; 🚇Ginza line to Nihombashi, exit C5)

Kaiten (sushi conveyor belt)

Nihonbashi Dashi Bar Hanare

JAPANESE ¥

9 🍴 MAP P40, F2

This casual restaurant from long-time producer (300-plus years!) of *katsuo-bushi* (dried bonito flakes), Ninben, naturally serves dishes that make use of the umami-rich ingredient. Set meals, with dishes such as hearty miso soups and *dashi takikokomi gohan* (rice steamed in stock), are good value, and healthy to boot. (日本橋だし場はなれ; ☎03-5205-8704; www.ninben.co.jp/hanare; 1st fl, Coredo Muromachi 2, 2-3-1 Nihombashi-Muromachi, Chūō-ku; set meals ¥1025-1950, dishes ¥650-1300; ⊙11am-2pm & 5-11pm; S Ginza line to Mitsukoshimae, exit A6)

Nemuro Hanamaru

SUSHI ¥

The port of Nemuro in northern Hokkaidō is where this popular sushi operation first started. At this branch, on the 4th floor of the KITTE mall (see 15 🍴 Map p40, D3), it's a self-serve *kaiten* sushi where the vinegared rice bites are delivered by rotating conveyor belt. The line here can often be very long but it's worth the wait for the quality and price . (根室花まる; ☎03-6269-9026; www.sushi-hanamaru.com; 4th fl, KITTE, 2-7-2 Marunouchi, Chiyoda-ku; sushi per plate ¥140-540; ⊙11am-10pm, to 9pm Sun; 🚃JR lines to Tokyo, Marunouchi south exit)

Tokyo Rāmen Street   RAMEN ¥

10 ✖ MAP P40, D3

Eight hand-picked *rāmen-ya* operate branches in this basement arcade on the Yaesu side of Tokyo Station (p41). All the major styles are covered – from *shōyu* (soy-sauce base) to *tsukemen* (cold noodles served on the side). Long lines form outside the most popular shops, but they tend to move quickly. (東京ラーメンストリート; www.tokyoeki-1bangai.co.jp/ramenstreet; basement, First Avenue, Tokyo Station, 1-9-1 Marunouchi, Chiyoda-ku; ramen from ¥800; ⏰7.30am-11.30pm; 🚊JR lines to Tokyo, Yaesu south exit)

Nihonbashi Tamai   JAPANESE ¥¥

11 ✖ MAP P40, F3

This Nihombashi stalwart specialises in *anago* (saltwater conger eel), which is cheaper and not endangered like its freshwater cousin *unagi*. The eels are prepared to perfection here, laid out in lacquerware boxes (a style known as *hakomeshi*) and served either grilled or boiled – you can sample both cooking styles by asking for half and half. (玉ゐ 本店; ☎03-3272-3227; www.anago-tamai.com; 2-9-9 Nihombashi, Chūō-ku; mains from ¥1450; ⏰11am-2.30pm & 5-9.30pm Mon-Fri, 11.30am-3.30pm & 4.30-9pm Sat & Sun; 🚇Ginza line to Nihonbashi, exit C4)

Suigian   👍

For an up-close and personal taster of traditional Japanese performing arts, including *nō* and *kyōgen* drama and courtly dances, make a reservation for one of three, 40-minute performances that take place at **Suigian** (水戯庵; Map p40, F2; ☎03-3527-9378; https://suigian.jp; basement, 2-5-10 Nihombashi-Muromachi, Chūō-ku; seating charge from ¥3800 plus 1 drink or food; ⏰11am-11.30pm, to 9pm Sun; 🚇Ginza line to Mitsukoshi-mae, exit A6). The small stage is backed by a beautiful painting of a pine tree, and surrounded by an intimate, sophisticated restaurant and bar.

Drinking

Chashitsu Kaboku   TEAHOUSE

12 ☕ MAP P40, C4

Run by famed Kyoto tea producer Ippōdō – which celebrated 300 years of business in 2017 – this teahouse is a fantastic place to experience the myriad pleasures of *o-cha* (green tea). It's also one of the few places that serves *koicha* (thick tea), which is even thicker than *matcha* (powdered green tea). Sets are accompanied by a pretty, seasonal *wagashi* (Japanese sweet). (茶室 嘉木; ☎03-6212-0202; www.ippodo-tea.co.jp; 3-1-1 Marunouchi, Chiyoda-ku; tea set ¥1080-2600; 🕐11am-7pm; 🚃JR Yamanote line to Yurakuchō, Tokyo International Forum exit)

Toyama Bar
BAR

13 🚇 MAP P40, E2

This slick counter bar offers a selection of sakes from 17 different Toyama breweries. A set of three 30mL cups costs a bargain ¥700 (90mL cups from ¥700 each). English tasting notes are available. It's part of the Nihonbashi Toyama-kan (日本橋とやま館), which promotes goods produced in Japan's northern Toyama Prefecture. Pick up a bottle of anything you like at the attached shop. (トヤマバー; 📞03-6262-2723; www.toyamakan.jp; 1-2-6 Nihombashi-muromachi, Chūō-ku; 🕐11am-9pm; 🚇Ginza line to Mitsukoshimae, exit B5)

Café & Meal MUJI, Yūrakuchō

REBECCA MILNER / LONELY PLANET ©

(marunouchi) House
BAR

14 🚇 MAP P40, D3

On the 7th floor of the Shin-Maru Building, this collection of nine bars and pubs is a popular after-work gathering spot. There's a wrap-around terrace, so many spots have outdoor seating. The views aren't sky-high; instead you feel curiously suspended among the office towers, hovering over Tokyo Station (p41) below. The bars often come together to hold joint events. (丸の内ハウス; 📞03-5218-5100; www.marunouchi-house.com; 7th fl, Shin-Maru Bldg, 1-5-1 Marunouchi, Chiyoda-ku; 🕐11am-4am Mon-Sat, to 11pm Sun; 📶; 🚃JR lines to Tokyo, Marunouchi north exit)

Shopping

KITTE
MALL

15 🔒 MAP P40, D3

This well-designed shopping mall at the foot of JP Tower incorporates the restored original facade of the **Tokyo Central Post Office** (東京中央郵便局; Map p40, D3; 📞03-3217-5231; https://map.japanpost.jp/p/search/dtl/300101615000/; 2-7-2 Marunouchi, Chiyoda-ku; 🕐9am-9pm Mon-Fri, to 7pm Sat & Sun). It is notable for its atrium, around which is arrayed a quality selection of craft-oriented Japanese-brand shops selling homewares, fashion, accessories and lifestyle goods. (📞03-3216-2811; www.jptower-kitte.jp; 2-7-2 Marunouchi, Chiyoda-ku; 🕐shops 11am-9pm Mon-Sat, to 8pm Sun, restaurants 11am-11pm, to 10pm

Sun; 🚃JR lines to Tokyo, Marunouchi south exit)

On the 3rd floor **Good Design Store Tokyo by Nohara** (📞03-5220-1007; http://gdst.nohara-inc.co.jp; 🕐11am-9pm, to 8pm Sun) showcases a fab selection of products that have gained Japan's Good Design Award.

Coredo Muromachi

MALL

16 🔒 MAP P40, E2

Spread over three buildings, this stylish development houses many shops from famous gourmet food purveyors, as well as reliable places to eat and drink. In Coredo Muromachi 3 are elegant fashion and homewares boutiques, including a branch of Muji. (コレド室町; www.mitsui-shopping-park.com/urban/muromach; 2-2-1 Nihombashi-Muromachi, Chūō-ku; 🕐most shops 10am-9pm; Ⓢ Ginza line to Mitsukoshi-mae, exit A4)

MUJI

HOMEWARES

17 🔒 MAP P40, D4

The flagship store of the famously understated brand sells elegant, simple clothing, accessories, homewares and food. There are scores of outlets across Tokyo, but the Yūrakuchō store, renovated in 2017, is the largest with the biggest range.

Department Stores

Tokyo's grandest and oldest department stores, **Mitsukoshi** (三越; Map p40, E2; 📞03-3241-3311; www.mitsukoshi.co.jp; 1-4-1 Nihombashi-Muromachi, Chūō-ku; 🕐10am-7pm; Ⓢ Ginza line to Mitsukoshimae, exit A2) and **Takashimaya** (高島屋; Map p40, E3; 📞03-6273 1467; www.takashimaya.co.jp/tokyo/store_information; 2-4-1 Nihombashi, Chūō-ku; 🕐10.30am-7.30pm; Ⓢ Ginza line to Nihombashi, Takashimaya exit), politely stand off against each other on either side of Nihombashi. Arrive at either at 10am for the bells and bows that accompany each day's opening.

It also offers tax-free shopping, bicycle rental (¥1080 per day from 10am to 8pm; passport required) and a great **cafeteria** (MealMUJI有楽町; 📞03-5208-8245; http://cafemeal.muji.com/jp; 2nd fl, 3-8-3 Marunouchi, Chiyoda-ku; meals ¥850-1200; 🕐10am-9pm; 🍴; 🚃JR Yamanote line to Yūrakuchō, Kyōbashi exit). (無印良品; 📞03-5208-8241; www.muji.com/jp/flagship/yurakucho/en; 3-8-3 Marunouchi, Chiyoda-ku; 🕐10am-9pm; 🚃JR Yamanote line to Yūrakuchō, Kyōbashi exit)

Explore ⊚

Ginza

Ginza is Tokyo's most polished neighbourhood, a luxury fashion centre resplendent with department stores, art galleries and exclusive restaurants; the city's principal kabuki theatre, Kabukiza, is here, too. Tokyo's main fish market may no longer be based at nearby Tsukiji, but this area remains packed with shops providing all you need to eat and make a great meal.

The Short List

○ **Tsukiji Market (p55)** Sample a delicious array of seafood and other delicious eats at this bustling market area.

○ **Kabukiza (p50)** Be dazzled by the Technicolor spectacle of kabuki drama.

○ **Hama-rikyū Onshi-teien (p55)** Sip green tea in this beautiful bayside garden.

○ **Okuno Building (p53)** Visit a 1932 apartment block crammed with tiny art galleries.

○ **Ginza Six (p60)** Empty your wallet in the area's biggest luxury mall.

Getting There & Around

🚃 The JR Yamanote line stops at Shimbashi Station and Yūrakuchō Station.

Ⓢ The Ginza, Hibiya and Marunouchi lines connect at Ginza Station. For Tsukiji, take either the Hibiya line to Tsukiji or the Ōedo line to Tsukijishijō.

Water Bus Connect between Hama-rikyū Onshi-teien and Asakusa or Odaiba by ferry.

Neighbourhood Map on p54

Ginza Six (p60) JOE_KITTIDATE / SHUTTERSTOCK ©

Top Experience 📷
Catch a kabuki show at Kabukiza

Dramatic, intensely visual kabuki is Japan's most recognised art form. It developed during the reign of the shogun and was shaped by the increasingly wealthy merchant class of Edo (old Tokyo under the shogun) – resulting in breathtaking costumes and elaborate stagecraft. Kabukiza (歌舞伎座) is Tokyo's kabuki theatre. Established in 1889, it was reconstructed in 2013 to incorporate a tower block and flamboyant facade (designed by Kuma Kengo).

◎ **MAP P54, D2**

📞 03-3545-6800

www.kabukiweb.net

4-12-15 Ginza, Chūō-ku

tickets ¥4000-20,000, for single acts ¥800-2000

🚉 Hibiya line to Higashi-Ginza, exit 3

The Plays

Kabuki developed over several centuries during the reign of the shogun, amassing a repertoire of popular themes, such as famous historical accounts, the conflict between love and loyalty, and stories of star-crossed love ending in double suicide. Chikamatsu Monzaemon (1653–1724) is kabuki's most famous playwright, even though he originally wrote most plays for bunraku puppetry.

The Performance

There is no pretence of reality in kabuki; it's ruled by aesthetics and plays to the senses rather than the intellect. Kabuki has been likened to a moving woodblock print, and when the actors pause in dramatic poses – called *mie* – the whole stage really does look fit to be framed.

The kabuki stage employs a number of unique devices, such as the *hanamichi* (the walkway that extends into the audience), which is used for dramatic entrances and exits. Naturally the best seats are those that line the *hanamichi*.

A full kabuki performance comprises three or four acts (usually from different plays) over an afternoon or an evening (typically 11am to 3.30pm or 4.30pm to 9pm), with long intervals between the acts.

If four-plus hours sounds too long, 90 sitting and 60 standing tickets are sold on the day for each single act. You'll be at the back of the auditorium but the views are still good.

The Actors

Kabuki actors train from childhood and descendants of the great Edo-era actors still grace the stage, as sons follow their fathers into the *yago* (kabuki acting house). These stars enjoy a celebrity on par with screen actors; some have earned the status of 'living treasure'. At pivotal moments in a performance, enthusiastic fans shout out the actor's *yago* – an act called *kakegoe*.

★ Top Tips

○ If you purchased a ticket online, look for the ticket dispensers in front of the theatre and in the basement passage from the subway station. Just insert the credit card you used to purchase the ticket.

○ Rent a headset for explanations in English; the recording begins 10 minutes before each act, with background information about the play.

○ Arrive at least 1½ hours before the start of the performance to be sure of getting a single-act ticket.

✖ Take a Break

It's tradition to eat a *bentō* (boxed meal) at the theatre during the intermission. Purchase one (around ¥1000) in the theatre, at stalls in the subway station, or in the food hall of nearby department store **Mitsukoshi** (三越; ☎ 03-3562-1111; http://mitsukoshi.mistore.jp/store/ginza; 4-6-16 Ginza, Chūō-ku; ⏱ 10.30am-8pm, restaurant fl 11am-11pm).

Walking Tour 🥾

Ginza Old & New

Ginza is a grand master of innovation and reinvention. This is where Tokyoites first encountered European-style architecture in the late 19th century. You could easily spend a full day in this classy district of old and new, discovering vintage gems alongside shiny contemporary structures.

Walk Facts

Start Bongen Coffee; Ⓢ Higashi-Ginza Station, exit A7

End Ginza Six; Ⓢ Ginza Station

Length 1km; two to three hours

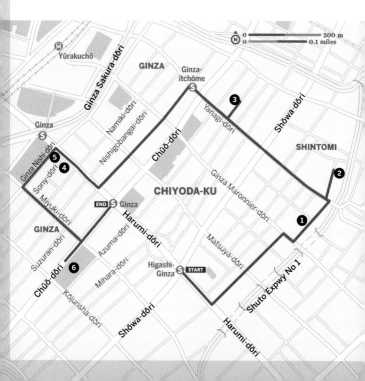

❶ Bongen Coffee

Start the day with a caffeine jolt from tiny **Bongen Coffee** (📞03-6264-3988; www.ginza-bongen.jp; 2-16-3 Ginza, Chūō-ku; ⏰10am-8pm; 📶), serving single-estate brews with side orders of *onigiri* (Japanese rice balls) or sandwiches of raisins and cream. Admire the spotlit bonsai tree behind the espresso machine.

❷ Morioka Shoten & Co

This tiny **bookshop** (森岡書店 銀座店; 📞03-3535-5020; Suzuki Bldg, 1–28–15 Ginza, Chūō-ku; ⏰1-8pm Tue-Sun) showcases a single title a week, be it a novel, a cookbook or an art tome, alongside an exhibition. However, the real reason for coming here is for the wonderful art deco architecture of the 1929 Suzuki Building, with its warm red-brick and decorative tile facade.

❸ Okuno Building Galleries

This 1932 apartment block (cutting edge for its time) is a retro time capsule, its seven floors packed with tiny boutiques and **galleries** (奥野ビル; 1-9-8 Ginza, Chūō-ku; ⏰most galleries noon-7pm). It's a fascinating place to explore with Escher-like staircases, an antique elevator shaft and an ever-changing selection of mini-exhibitions.

❹ Ginza Maison Hermès Le Forum

Renzo Piano was the architect of this skinny building constructed from specially made glass blocks. Light floods into its 8th-floor **gallery** (📞03-3569-3300; www.maisonhermes.jp; 8F Maison Hermès, 5-4-1 Ginza, Chūō-ku; admission free; ⏰11am-8pm, to 7pm Sun) that hosts around three different contemporary art shows per year, usually showcasing works of French artists.

❺ Ginza Sony Park

Below ground at this innovative park (p60) are four levels hosting a variety of pop-up events and places to eat and drink. Head to the information desk (level B1, open 10am to 8pm) to find out what's on and to play with Sony's super-cute robot dog Aibo.

❻ Ginza Six

Find a new outfit or a classy souvenir at the many shops in this slick mall (p60), check out its digital-art waterfall, then take a breather in its rooftop garden, which provides a superb view of the area.

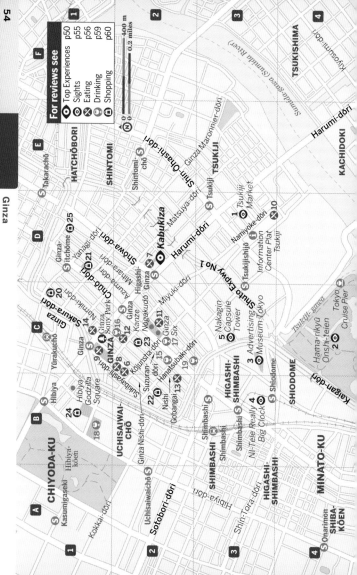

For reviews see
- Top Experiences p50
- Sights p55
- Eating p56
- Drinking p59
- Shopping p60

0 ___ 400 m
0 ___ 0.2 miles

CHIYODA-KU

Kasumigaseki

Hibiya-kōen

Hibiya
Godzilla Square

UCHISAIWAI-CHŌ

Ginza Nishi-dōri

Uchisaiwaichō

Sotobori-dōri

Kokkai-dōri

Hibiya-dōri

Shin-Tora-dōri

HIGASHI-SHIMBASHI

SHIMBASHI

Shimbashi

Ni-Tele Really 4
Big Clock

MINATO-KU

HIGASHI-SHIMBASHI

SHIBA-KŌEN

Onarimon

Kaigan-dōri

Tokyo Cruise Pier

Tokyo
Cruise Pier

Hama-rikyū
Onshi-teien 2

SHIODOME

Advertising
Museum Tokyo 3

Nakagin
Capsule
Tower 5

Shuto Expwy No 1

Miyuki-dōri

HIGASHI-
SHIMBASHI

Hanatsubaki-dōri

Nishi
Gobangai 13

Suzuran-dōri

Sukiyabashi-dōri

Kōjunsha-dōri

22

Ginza Six 17

19

Ginza 15

Ginza 11
Nozakudō 23

Kanze

Ginza 12

Ginza Sony Park 14

GINZA 16 8
6
10 7
9

Yūrakuchō

Namiki-dōri

Chūō-dōri

Ginza
Sakura-dōri

Ginza-dōri 20

Ginza
1chōme 21 25

Yanagi-dōri

Azuma-dōri

Mihara-dōri

Shōwa-dōri

Higashi-
Ginza

Tsukiji-
shijō

Shintomi-
chō

Takarachō

HATCHOBORI

SHINTOMI

Shin-Ohashi-dōri

Ginza Maronnier-dōri

Kabukiza

Harumi-dōri

Matsuya-dōri

TSUKIJI

Tsukiji

Tsukiji
Market

Namiyoke-dōri

Tsukiji
Information
Center Plat 10

Sumida-gawa (Sumida River)

Harumi-dōri

TSUKISHIMA

KACHIDOKI

Kiyosumi-dōri

18

24

Sights

Tsukiji Market

MARKET

1 MAP P54, D3

Tokyo's main wholesale market may have moved to Toyosu, but there are many reasons to visit its old home. The tightly packed rows of vendors (which once formed the Outer Market) hawk market and culinary-related goods, such as dried fish, seaweed, kitchen knives, rubber boots and crockery. It's also a fantastic place to eat, with great street food and a huge concentration of small restaurants and cafes, most specialising in seafood.

Enjoy a reasonably priced, delicious bowl of *ikura* (salmon roe) over rice at **Tadokoro Shokuhin** (田所食品; ☎03-3541-7754; 4-9-11 Tsukiji, Chūō-ku; noodles ¥700, rice bowls from ¥1500; ⏰7am-3pm Mon, Tue & Thu-Sat).

For crockery, fine-quality kitchen knives and kitchen implements, search out **Tsukiji Hitachiya** (つきじ常陸屋; ☎03-3541-1296; 4-14-18 Tsukiji, Chūō-ku; ⏰8am-3pm Mon-Sat, 10am-2pm Sun).

Pick up an English map of the market from **Information Centre Plat Tsukiji** (ぷらっと築地; Map p54, D3; ☎03-6264-1925; 4-16-2 Tsukiji, Chūō-ku; ⏰8am-2pm Mon-Sat, from 10am Sun), where you can also buy unique Tsukiji souvenirs. (場外市場, Jōgai Shijō; www.tsukiji.or.jp; 6-chōme Tsukiji, Chūō-ku; ⏰mostly 5am-2pm, some shops closed Sun & Wed; **S** Hibiya line to Tsukiji, exit 1)

Hama-rikyū Onshi-teien

GARDENS

2 MAP P54, C4

This beautiful garden, one of Tokyo's finest, is all that remains of a shogunate palace that was also an outer fort for Edo Castle. The main features are a large duck pond with an island that's home to a functioning tea pavilion, **Nakajima no Ochaya** (中島の御茶屋; 1-1 Hama-rikyū Onshi-teien, Chūō-ku; tea ¥510 or ¥720; ⏰9am-4.30pm), as well as three other teahouses and wonderfully manicured trees (black pine, Japanese apricot, hydrangeas etc), some of which are hundreds of years old. (浜離宮恩賜庭園, Detached Palace Garden; ☎03-3541-0200; www.tokyo-park.or.jp/teien; 1-1 Hama-rikyū-teien, Chūō-ku; adult/child ¥300/free; ⏰9am-5pm; **S** Ōedo line to Shiodome, exit A1)

Advertising Museum Tokyo

MUSEUM

3 MAP P54, C3

If you see advertising as art, this museum is a spectacle. Run by Dentsu, Japan's largest advertising agency, this fine collection runs from woodblock-printed handbills from the Edo period via sumptuous art nouveau and art deco Meiji- and Taishō-era works to the best of today. There's English signage throughout, and touch screens to view many classic TV ads. (アド・ミュージアム東京; ☎03-6218-2500; www.admt.jp; basement, Caretta Bldg, 1-8-2 Higashi-Shimbashi, Minato-ku;

Godzilla Spotting

Godzilla's assault on Tokyo continues apace: first there was the Godzilla Head (p119) that appeared on the Toho building in Shinjuku; and now a 3m-tall statue can be found, poised for attack, in what has been redubbed **Hibiya Godzilla Square** (日比谷 ゴジラスクエア; Map p54, B1; Hibiya Chanter, 1-2-2 Yūrakuchō, Chiyoda-ku; S Hibiya line to Hibiya, exit A4). It's a model of the monster that appears in the 2016 film *Shin Godzilla*.

admission free; ⏱11am-6pm Tue-Sat; S Ōedo line to Shiodome, Shimbashi exit)

NI-Tele Really Big Clock

PUBLIC ART

4 ◉ MAP P54, B3

Studio Ghibli's animation director Miyazaki Hayao collaborated with sculptor Shachimaru Kunio on this fantastic, steampunk-style timepiece beside the entrance to Nippon Television Tower. Four times daily (with an extra morning show on weekends), various automaton elements spring to life as the clock strikes the hour and plays a jolly tune. (日テレ大時計; 1-6-1 Higashi-Shimbashi, Minato-ku; admission free; ⏱operates at noon, 3pm, 6pm & 8pm, also 10am Sat & Sun; 🚃JR lines to Shimbashi, Shiodome exit)

Nakagin Capsule Tower

ARCHITECTURE

5 ◉ MAP P54, C3

This early-1970s building by Kurokawa Kishō is a seminal work of Metabolism, an experimental architecture movement to create fluid, more organic structures. The tower is made up of self-contained pods around a central core that are meant to be replaced every 20 years. Long story short: they were never replaced and the building is just shy of being condemned, though remaining residents (and many more fans) have been campaigning to save it. Entry is by tour only. (中銀カプセ ルタワー; www.nakagincapsuletower. com/nakagincapsuletour; 8-16-10 Ginza, Chūō-ku; tours in Japanese/ English ¥3000/4000; S Ōedo line to Tsukijishijō, exit A3)

Eating

Ginza Kazami

RAMEN ¥

6 ✖ MAP P54, C2

Go down the alley in the middle of a Ginza block to find this small shop specialising in ramen. Its bowl of choice is *sake kasu noko soba,* which has a broth flavoured with sake lees. (銀座風見; 📞03-3572-0737; 6-4-14 Ginza, Chūō-ku; ramen from ¥950; ⏱11.30am-3pm & 5.30-10pm Mon-Sat; S Ginza line to Ginza, exits C2 & C3)

Ain Soph

VEGAN ¥¥

7  MAP P54, D2

Truly vegan restaurants are few and far between in Tokyo and ones that make so much effort over their food as Ain Soph are even rarer. Thank heavens then for this stylish place (bookings are essential for dinner) that serves delicious *bentō*-box meals, vegan-cheese fondue, smoothies and fluffy American-style pancakes. (☏03-6228-4241; www.ain-soph. jp; 4-12-1 Ginza, Chūō-ku; mains from ¥1680, bentō boxes & set menus lunch/dinner from ¥2480/3250; ⏲11.30am-10pm Wed-Mon; ⓢAsakusa or Hibiya line to Higashi-Ginza, exit A7)

Ginza Sato Yosuke

NOODLES ¥¥

8  MAP P54, C2

A speciality of Akita Prefecture, *inaniwa* wheat noodles have been made by seven generations of the Sato family. As you'll be able to tell from the glossy, silky textured results, they've pretty much got it down to perfection. Sample the noodles in a hot chicken broth or cold dipping sauces such as sesame and miso or green curry. (銀座 佐藤養助; ☏03-6215-6211; www.sato-yoske.co.jp/en/shop/ginza; 6-4-17 Ginza, Chūō-ku; noodles from ¥1300; ⏲11.30am-3pm & 5-10pm; ⓢMarunouchi line to Ginza, exit C2)

Apollo

GREEK ¥¥

9  MAP P54, C1

Ginza's glittering lights are the dazzling backdrop to this ace import from Sydney with its delicious take on modern Greek cuisine. The Mediterranean flavours come through strongly in dishes such as grilled octopus and fennel salad, taramasalata, and lamb shoulder with lemon and Greek yoghurt. Portions are large and meant for sharing. (☏03-6264-5220; www.theapollo.jp; 11th fl, Tōkyū Plaza Ginza, 5-2-1 Ginza, Chūō-ku; mains ¥1680-5980; ⏲11am-11pm; ⓢGinza line to Ginza, exits C2 & C3)

Trattoria Tsukiji Paradiso!

ITALIAN ¥¥

10  MAP P54, D3

Paradise for food lovers, indeed. This charming, aqua-painted trattoria serves seafood pasta dishes that will make you want to lick the plate clean. Its signature

Tempura

Ginza Promenade

Go for a stroll along Chūō-dōri each weekend, when a long section of the road is traffic-free from noon to 5pm (until 6pm, April to September).

linguine is packed with shellfish in a scrumptious tomato, chilli and garlic sauce. Lunch (from ¥980) is a bargain, but you'll need to queue; book for dinner. The menu is in Japanese and Italian. (トラットリア・築地パラディーゾ; ☑03-3545-5550; www.tsukiji-paradiso.com; 6-27-3 Tsukiji, Chūō-ku; mains ¥1500-3600; ⏰11am-2pm & 6-10pm Thu-Tue; ⑤Hibiya line to Tsukiji, exit 2)

Maru   JAPANESE ¥¥

11 ❌ MAP P54, C2

In the evenings Maru offers a contemporary take on *kaiseki* (Japanese haute cuisine) fine dining. The chefs are young and inventive, and the appealing space is dominated by a long, wooden, open kitchen counter across which you can watch them work. The good-value lunches offer a choice of *yaki-zakana* (grilled fish) dishes or *higawari teishoku* (the day's special). (銀座maru; ☑03-5537-7420; www.maru-mayfont.jp/ginza; 2nd fl, Ichigo Ginza 612 Bldg, 6-12-15 Ginza, Chūō-ku; lunch/dinner from ¥1100/4800; ⏰11.30am-2pm & 5.30-9pm Mon-Sat; ⑤Ginza line to Ginza, exit A3)

Tempura Kondō   TEMPURA ¥¥¥

12 ❌ MAP P54, C2

Nobody in Tokyo does tempura vegetables like chef Kondō Fumiō. The carrots are julienned to a fine floss; the corn is pert, juicy; and the sweet potato is comfort food at its finest. Courses include seafood, too. Lunch service at noon or 1.30pm; last dinner booking at 8pm. Reserve ahead. (てんぷら近藤; ☑03-5568-0923; 9th fl, Sakaguchi Bldg, 5-5-13 Ginza, Chūō-ku; lunch/dinner course from ¥6500/11,000; ⏰noon-3pm & 5-10pm Mon-Sat; ⑤Ginza line to Ginza, exit B5)

Kyūbey   SUSHI ¥¥¥

13 ❌ MAP P54, B2

Since 1935, Kyūbey's quality and presentation have won it a moneyed and celebrity clientele. Despite the cachet, this is a relaxed restaurant. The friendly owner Imada-san speaks excellent English, as do some of his team of talented chefs, who will make and serve your sushi, piece by piece. The ¥8000 lunchtime *omakase* (chef's selection) is great value. (久兵衛; ☑03-3571-6523; www.kyubey.jp; 8-7-6 Ginza, Chūō-ku; set meals lunch/dinner from ¥4400/11,000; ⏰11.30am-2pm & 5-10pm Mon-Sat; ⑤Ginza line to Shimbashi, exit 3)

Bird Land   YAKITORI ¥¥¥

14 ❌ MAP P54, C1

This is as suave as it gets for gourmet grilled chicken. Chefs in whites behind a U-shaped counter dispense *yakitori* in all shapes, sizes, colours and organs – don't pass up the dainty serves of liver pâté or the tiny cup of chicken soup. Pair it with wine from the extensive list. Enter beneath Suit Company. Reservations recommended. (バードランド; ☑03-5250-1081; www.ginza-birdland. sakura.ne.jp; 4-2-15 Ginza, Chūō-ku; dishes ¥500-2000, set meals from ¥6300; ☺5-9.30pm Tue-Sat; Ⓢ Ginza line to Ginza, exit C6)

Drinking

Ginza Music Bar   COCKTAIL BAR

15 Ⓜ MAP P54, C2

A superb sound system showcases the 3000-plus vinyl collection that ranges from the likes of cool classic jazz to contemporary electronica. There are deep-blue walls and comfy seats in which to enjoy inventive cocktails (starting from ¥1400), such as a *matcha* and wasabi martini. (☑03-3572-3666; www.ginzamusicbar.com; 4F Brownplace, 7-8-13 Ginza, Chūō-ku; cover charge after midnight ¥1000; ☺6pm-4am Mon-Sat; Ⓢ Ginza line to Shimbashi, exits 1 & 3)

Cha Ginza   TEAHOUSE

16 Ⓜ MAP P54, C2

Take a pause for afternoon tea (¥700 to ¥1400) at this slick contemporary tea salon. The menu is seasonal, but will likely include a cup of perfectly prepared *matcha* (powdered green tea) and a small sweet or two, or a

choice of *sencha* (premium green tea). The ground-floor shop sells top-quality teas from various growing regions in Japan. (茶・銀座; ☑03-3571-1211; www.uogashi-meicha.co.jp; 5-5-6 Ginza, Chūō-ku; ☺teahouse noon-5pm Tue-Sat, shop 11am-6pm Tue-Sat; Ⓢ Ginza line to Ginza, exit B3)

Ginza Lion   BEER HALL

17 Ⓜ MAP P54, C2

So what if Sapporo's beers are not among the best you can quaff in Tokyo? The gorgeous art deco design, including glass mosaic murals, at Japan's oldest beer hall dating to 1934 is to die for. The oom-pah-pah atmosphere with waiters ferrying frothy mugs and plates of Bavarian-style sausages to the tables is also priceless. (銀座ライオン; ☑050-5269-7095; https://ginzalion.net; 7-9-20 Ginza, Chūō-ku; ☺11.30am-11pm, to 10.30pm Sun; Ⓢ Ginza line to Ginza, exit A2)

Old Imperial Bar   BAR

18 Ⓜ MAP P54, B1

One of the few parts of the Imperial Hotel to feature some of the designs and materials used in Frank Lloyd Wright's 1923 building (note the architectural drawing behind the cash desk). It's a dimly lit, classy place to enjoy a cocktail (from ¥1580) or a shot of its signature 21-year-old Scotch whisky blend (¥2400). (Mezzanine, Main Bldg, Imperial Hotel, 1-1-1 Uchisaiwai-chō, Chiyoda-ku;

Ginza Rebooted

With other commercial areas of Tokyo smartening up their act, Ginza – long the city's ritziest shopping destination – has been going all out to update its retail infrastructure and surroundings. **Ginza Six** (Map p54, C2; ☎03-6891-3390; http://ginza6.tokyo; 6-10-1 Ginza, Chūō-ku; ⏰10am-10pm; Ⓢ Ginza line to Ginza, exit A2), the area's biggest luxury mall, opened in April 2017, and includes international and local top-brand shops, restaurants, a 4000-sq-metre rooftop garden with great views and **Kanze Nōgakudō** (観世能楽堂; Map p54, C2; ☎03-6274-6579; www.kanze.net; Ginza Six B3, 6-10-1 Ginza, Chūō-ku; Ⓢ Ginza line to Ginza, exit A2), a theatre specialising in *nō* dramas. Digital and contemporary art feature in the public areas.

On the corner of Sukiyabashi Crossing is the innovative public space **Ginza Sony Park** (Map p54, C1; 銀座ソニーパーク; www.ginzasonypark.jp; 5-3-1 Ginza, Chūō-ku; admission free; ⏰5am-midnight; Ⓢ Ginza, Hibiya or Marunouchi lines to Ginza, exit B9). At ground level greenery flourishes, while below ground there are four levels hosting a variety of pop-up events and places to eat and drink. Sony is currently building its new showroom here.

⏰11.30am-midnight; Ⓢ Hibiya line to Hibiya, exit A13)

Cafe de l'Ambre   CAFE

19 🚇 MAP P54, C2

The sign over the door here reads 'Coffee Only' but, oh, what a selection (coffee from ¥700). Sekiguchi Ichiro started the business in 1948, sourcing and roasting aged beans from all over the world – he ran the place until close to his death at 103 in 2018. It's dark, retro and classic Ginza. (カフェ・ド・ランブル; ☎03-3571-1551; www.cafedelambre.com; 8-10-15 Ginza, Chūō-ku; ⏰noon-10pm Mon-Sat, to 7pm Sun; 🚇 Ginza line to Ginza, exit A4)

Shopping

Akomeya   FOOD

20 🅐 MAP P54, C1

Rice is at the core of Japanese cuisine and drink. This stylish store sells not only many types of the grain but also products made from it (such as sake), a vast range of quality cooking ingredients, and a choice collection of kitchen, home and bath items. (アコメヤ; ☎03-6758-0271; www.akomeya.jp; 2-2-6 Ginza, Chūō-ku; ⏰shop 11am-8pm Sun-Thu, to 9pm Fri & Sat, restaurant 11am-10pm; Ⓢ Yūrakuchō line to Ginza-itchōme, exit 4)

Itōya

ARTS & CRAFTS

21 MAP P54, D1

Explore the nine floors (plus several more in the nearby annex) of stationery at this famed, century-old Ginza establishment. There are everyday items (such as notebooks and greeting cards) and luxuries (fountain pens and Italian leather agendas). You'll also find *washi* (Japanese handmade paper), *tenu-gui* (beautifully hand-dyed thin cotton towels) and *furoshiki* (wrapping cloths). (伊東屋; ☑03-3561-8311; www.ito-ya.co.jp; 2-7-15 Ginza, Chūō-ku; ☺10.30am-8pm Mon-Sat, to 7pm Sun; ⑤Ginza line to Ginza, exit A13)

Takumi

ARTS & CRAFTS

22 MAP P54, B2

You're unlikely to find a more elegant selection of traditional folk crafts, including toys, textiles and ceramics from around Japan. Ever thoughtful, this shop also encloses information detailing the origin and background of the pieces if you make a purchase. (たくみ; ☑03-3571-2017; www.ginza-takumi.co.jp; 8-4-2 Ginza, Chūō-ku; ☺11am-7pm Mon-Sat; ⑤Ginza line to Shimbashi, exit 5)

Dover Street Market Ginza

FASHION & ACCESSORIES

23 MAP P54, C2

A department store as envisioned by Kawakubo Rei (of Comme des Garçons), DSM has seven floors of avant-garde brands, including several Japanese labels and

everything in the Comme des Garçons line-up. The quirky art installations alone make it worth the visit. (DSM; ☑03-6228-5080; http://ginza.doverstreetmarket.com; 6-9-5 Ginza, Chūō-ku; ☺11am-8pm; ⑤Ginza line to Ginza, exit A2)

Tokyo Midtown Hibiya

MALL

24 MAP P54, B1

This classy mixed-use complex, which opened in 2018, has a good assortment of fashionable boutiques as well as the 11-screen Toho multiplex. Check out the stylised **Hibiya Central Market** on the 3rd floor, which is set up like an old-fashioned town shopping street. (東京ミッドタウン日比谷; ☑03-5157-1251; www.hibiya.tokyo-midtown.com; 1-1-2 Yūrakuchō, Chiyoda-ku; ☺11am-9pm, restaurants to 11pm; ⑤Hibiya line to Hibiya, exit A11)

Antique Mall Ginza

ANTIQUES

25 MAP P54, D1

At this subterranean market of antique and retro goods, you can pick up anything from old lacquerware and pottery to beautifully embroidered obi (the broad belt of a kimono) and jewellery. There are also some European pieces. Some shops are willing to negotiate prices. (アンティークモール銀座; ☑03-3535-2115; www.antiques-jp.com; 1-13-1 Ginza, Chūō-ku; ☺11am-7pm; ⑤Yūrakuchō line to Ginza-itchōme, exit A10)

Top Experience 📷

Get arty at teamLab Borderless

Opened in 2018, digital art collective teamLab created 60 installations for this museum that blurs the boundary between art and the viewer: many works are interactive. Not sure how? That's the point – approach the installations, move and touch them (or just stand still), and see how they react. There is no suggested route; teamLab Borderless is all about exploration.

📞 03-6406-3949

https://borderless.
teamlab.art

1-3-8 Aomi, Kōtō-ku

adult/child ¥3200/1000

🕑 10am-7pm Mon-Thu & Sun, to 9pm Fri & Sat, closed 2nd & 4th Tue of the month

🚉 Yurikamome line to Aomi

The Crystal World

Each room here feels like a discreet world – and wandering through the museum feels a bit like being inside a fantasy role-playing game. Inside the maze-like Crystal World, strands of shimmering light extend from floor to ceiling like disco stalagmites. Download the teamLab app ahead of time and you can set the lights in motion according to your mood.

Forest of Lamps

Many of the artworks here are optimised for photography, none more so than the magical Forest of Lamps. Approach one of the Venetian-glass lamps and watch it bloom into colour, setting off a chain reaction. Only a limited number of people are allowed in for a few minutes at a time. As this is among the most popular installations, you'll likely have to queue for it.

Athletics Forest

The collection of installations on the 2nd floor is designed with kids in mind – but grown-ups can join in, too. Jump up and down on a bouncy plain and see your energy transformed into expanding stars. Add colour to a drawing of an animal or insect and watch as it is born into an animated creature – then follow it on its course along the crags and divots of this playful indoor landscape.

En Teahouse

Stop for a cup of tea (¥500) at this digitally enhanced teahouse and see flowers come to life in your teacup; the petals blow away in the breeze when you've finished. And while you're here, don't miss the digital calligraphy installation of an *ensō*, a circle drawn in one stroke and a classic symbol of Zen Buddhism.

★ Top Tips

o Buy tickets in advance online, as they often sell out.

o Some of the installations have mirrored floors; for this reason we recommend wearing trousers. Trainers are a good idea, too.

o There are no mini-mum age require-ments; however, keep in mind the museum is dark and often crowded. Prams must be parked at the entrance.

✕ Take a Break

Adjacent shopping mall **Venus Fort** (ヴィーナスフォート; 📞03-3599-0700; www. venusfort.co.jp; 1-3-15 Aomi, Kōtō-ku; ⏰10am-9pm) has a food court with plenty of family-friendly options.

★ Getting There

🚃 Take the Yurikamome line from Shimbashi or Shiodome to Aomi. You can also take the Rinkai line from JR Ōsaki Station to Tokyo Teleport Station (exit A), but the walk to the museum is longer.

Explore ◈
Roppongi, Akasaka & Around

Roppongi offers several excellent art museums as well as legendary nightlife. Nearby is the iconic Tokyo Tower and some venerable temples. A short walk northeast, Akasaka is home to upmarket watering holes, a major Shintō shrine and an imperial palace.

The Short List

○ **Mori Art Museum (p67)** *See contemporary art and Tokyo's urban panorama atop Roppongi Hills' Mori Tower.*

○ **21_21 Design Sight (p70)** *View cutting-edge art, architecture and design ideas in a Tadao Ando– designed building.*

○ **Zōjō-ji (p71)** *Visit venerable temple with Tokyo Tower in the background.*

○ **National Art Center Tokyo (p70)** *Experience curvy architecture and top-notch exhibitions at building designed by Kurokawa Kishō.*

○ **Hie-jinja (p70)** *Approach this venerable hilltop shrine via a tunnel of red torii (gates).*

Getting There & Around

Ⓢ The Hibiya and Ōedo subway lines run through Roppongi. The Ōedo line can also be used to access Tokyo Tower and the Shiba-kōen area. Nogizaka on the Chiyoda line is directly connected to the National Art Center Tokyo. For Akasaka, the Yūrakuchō, Hanzōmon, Namboku, Chiyoda, Marunouchi and Ginza subway lines all converge in and around Akasaka.

Neighbourhood Map on p68

Zōjō-ji (p71) KUREMO / SHUTTERSTOCK ®

Top Experience 📷
Do it all at Roppongi Hills

The postmodern Roppongi Hills (六本木ヒルズ) mall covers more than 11 hectares and is home to a contemporary art museum, a sky-high observatory, shops galore, dozens of restaurants and even a formal Japanese garden. It's imposing, upmarket and polarising – an architectural marvel, a grand vision realised or a crass shrine to conspicuous consumption? Explore this urban maze and decide for yourself.

◎ **MAP P68, B5**

📞 03-6406-6000

www.roppongihills.com

6-chōme Roppongi, Minato-ku

🕐 11am-11pm

Ⓢ Hibiya line to Roppongi, exit 1

Mori Art Museum

Atop Mori Tower, this gigantic **gallery space**
(森美術館; www.mori.art.museum; 52nd fl, Mori
Tower, Roppongi Hills, 6-10-1 Roppongi, Minato-ku;
adult/child ¥1800/600; ⏱10am-10pm Wed-Mon, to
5pm Tue, inside Sky Deck 10am-10pm) sports high
ceilings, a broad view and thematic programs
that continue to live up to the hype. Contemporary exhibitions are beautifully presented and
include superstars of the art world from both
Japan and abroad. Look out for the museum's
triennial exhibition **Roppongi Crossing**, which
showcases up-and-coming Japanese artists.

Tokyo City View

Admission to the Mori Art Museum is shared with
Tokyo City View (東京シティビュー; ☏03-6406-
6652; adult/child ¥1800/600; ⏱10am-11pm Mon-Thu
& Sun, to 1am Fri & Sat), the observatory that wraps
itself around the 52nd floor, 250m high. The view
is spectacular at night. Weather permitting, you
can also pop out to the rooftop Sky Deck (additional adult/child ¥500/300; 11am to 8pm).

Public Art

The open-air plaza near the street entrance
is the home of one of Louise Bourgeois' giant
Maman spider sculptures. It has an amusing
way of messing with the scale of the buildings,
especially in photos. There are other sculptures,
paintings and installations – including works by
Miyajima Tatsuo and Cai Guo-Qiang.

Mohri Garden & Sakurazaka-kōen

Mohri Garden (毛利庭園, Mōri-teien) is the mall's
Edo-style strolling garden, with meandering
paths and a central pond. When juxtaposed with
the gleaming towers, the garden creates a fascinating study of luxury then and now.

Young children will love **Sakurazaka-kōen**
(さくら坂公園; www.city.minato.tokyo.jp/shisetsu/
koen/azabu/06.html; 6-16-46 Roppongi, Minato-ku;
admission free; 👶); South Korean artist Choi
Jeong-Hwa designed the dazzlingly colourful
robot-themed sculptures and play areas here.

★ Top Tips

○ Save your ticket stub from the Mori Art Museum to get discounted admission at the Suntory Museum of Art or the National Art Center Tokyo.

○ Unlike most museums, the Mori Art Museum is open late – until 10pm daily except Tuesday.

○ Keep an eye out for events, especially in summer, at Roppongi Hills Arena, an open-air space nestled in the middle of the complex.

✗ Take a Break

Start the day with breakfast or brunch at **Bricolage Bread & Co** (☏03-6804-3350; www.bricolage bread.com; 6-15-1 Roppongi, Minato-ku; mains ¥900-1600; ⏱9am-7.30pm Tue-Sun), just off leafy Keyaki-zaka. It's a collaboration between coffee shop Fuglen, Michelin-starred restaurant L'effervescence and Osaka-based bakery Le Sucré Coeur.

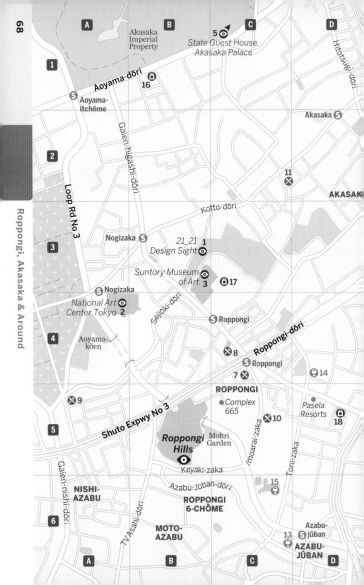

A
B
C
D

1

Akasaka
Imperial
Property

State Guest House,
Akasaka Palace
5

Aoyama-dōri

16

Ⓢ Aoyama-
itchōme

Akasaka Ⓢ

2

Galen-higashi-dōri

Loop Rd No 3

11
✕

AKASAKA

Kotto-dōri

3

Nogizaka Ⓢ

21_21 **1**
Design Sight ⊙

Suntory Museum
of Art **3**
⊙
17

Ⓢ Nogizaka

National Art ⊙
Center Tokyo **2**

Seijōki-dōri

Ⓢ Roppongi

Roppongi-dōri

4

Aoyama-
kōen

✕ **8**
Ⓢ Roppongi

14 🏺

7 ✕

ROPPONGI

✕ **9**

Shuto Expwy No 3

● Complex
665

✕ **10**

Pasela
Resorts

18

Roppongi
Hills
⊙

Mohri
Garden

Imoarai-zaka

Torii-zaka

5

Keyaki-zaka

15
🏺

Galen-nishi-dōri

Azabu-Jūban-dōri

**NISHI-
AZABU**

**ROPPONGI
6-CHŌME**

TV Asahi-dōri

**MOTO-
AZABU**

Azabu-
Ⓢ jūban

13 🏺
**AZABU-
JŪBAN**

6

Hitotsugi-dōri

A
B
C
D

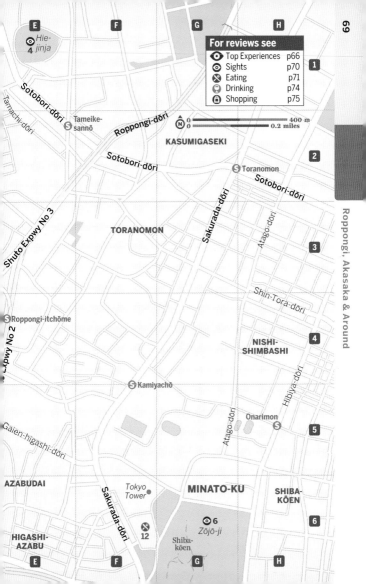

For reviews see

◉	Top Experiences	p66
◉	Sights	p70
✖	Eating	p71
🍷	Drinking	p74
🛍	Shopping	p75

Hie-jinja 4

Sotobori-dōri
Tamachi-dōri
Tameike-sannō
Roppongi-dōri
Sotobori-dōri

KASUMIGASEKI

N 0 ——— 400 m
0 ——— 0.2 miles

Toranomon
Sakurada-dōri
Sotobori-dōri
Atago-dōri

TORANOMON

Shuto Expwy No 3

Shin-Tora-dōri

Roppongi-itchōme

Expwy No 2

NISHI-SHIMBASHI

Kamiyachō

Gaien-higashi-dōri

Atago-dōri

Onarimon

Hibiya-dōri

AZABUDAI

Sakurada-dōri

Tokyo Tower

MINATO-KU

SHIBA-KŌEN

HIGASHI-AZABU

12

Zōjō-ji 6

Shiba-kōen

Sights

21_21 Design Sight MUSEUM

1 ◉ MAP P68, B3

An exhibition and discussion space dedicated to all forms of design, the 21_21 Design Sight acts as a beacon for local art enthusiasts, whether they be designers themselves or simply onlookers. The striking concrete and glass building, bursting out of the ground at sharp angles, was designed by Pritzker Prize–winning architect Tadao Ando. (21_21デザインサイト; ☎03-3475-2121; www.2121designsight. jp; Tokyo Midtown, 9-7-6 Akasaka, Minato-ku; adult/child ¥1100/free; ⏱11am-7pm Wed-Mon; Ⓢ Ōedo line to Roppongi, exit 8)

National Art Center Tokyo MUSEUM

2 ◉ MAP P68, A4

Designed by Kurokawa Kishō, this architectural beauty has no permanent collection, but boasts the country's largest exhibition space for visiting shows, which have included titans such as Renoir and Modigliani. Apart from exhibitions, a visit here is recommended to admire the building's awesome undulating glass facade, its cafes atop giant inverted cones and the great gift shop **Souvenir from Tokyo** (スーベニアフロムトーキョー; ☎03-6812 9933; www.souvenir-fromtokyo.jp; basement, National Art Center Tokyo, 7-22-2 Roppongi, Minato-ku; ⏱10am-6pm Sat-Mon,

Wed & Thu, to 8pm Fri; Ⓢ Chiyoda line to Nogizaka, exit 6). (国立新美術館; ☎03-5777-8600; www.nact.jp; 7-22-1 Roppongi, Minato-ku; admission varies by exhibition; ⏱10am-6pm Wed, Thu & Sun-Mon, to 8pm Fri & Sat; Ⓢ Chiyoda line to Nogizaka, exit 6)

Suntory Museum of Art MUSEUM

3 ◉ MAP P68, B3

Since its original 1961 opening, the Suntory Museum of Art has subscribed to an underlying philosophy of lifestyle art. Rotating exhibitions focus on the beauty of useful things: Japanese ceramics, lacquerware, glass, dyeing, weaving and such. Its current Tokyo Midtown (p75) digs, designed by architect Kengo Kuma, are both understated and breathtaking. (サントリー美術館; ☎03-3479-8600; www.suntory.com/sma; 4th fl, Tokyo Midtown, 9-7-4 Akasaka, Minato-ku; admission varies, child free; ⏱10am-6pm Sun-Wed, to 8pm Fri & Sat; Ⓢ Ōedo line to Roppongi, exit 8)

Hie-jinja SHINTO SHRINE

4 ◉ MAP P68, E1

Enshrining the deity of sacred Mt Hiei, northeast of Kyoto, this hilltop shrine has been the protector shrine of Edo-jō (Edo Castle), now the Imperial Palace (p36), since it was first built in 1478. It's an attractive place best approached by the tunnel of red *torii* on the hill's western side. There are also escalators up the hill from Tameike-sannō. (日枝神社; ☎03-3581-2471; www.hiejinja. net; 2-10-5 Nagatachō, Chiyoda-ku;

admission free; ⏰5am-6pm Apr-Sep, 6am-5pm Oct-Mar; Ⓢ Ginza line to Tameike-sannō, exits 5 & 7)

State Guest House, Akasaka Palace
PALACE

5 ◉ MAP P68, C1

Check online for the opening schedule and somewhat complex admission details for this imperial palace and garden. Outside it's a dead ringer for London's Buckingham Palace. Inside the tour route passes through four grandly decorated rooms – the most impressive being the **Kacho-no-Ma** (Room of Flowers and Birds), with Japanese ash panels inset with cloisonné panels – plus the entrance hall and main staircase. (迎賓館, 赤坂離宮; ☏03-3478-1111; www.geihinkan.go.jp/en/akasaka; 2-1-1, Moto-Akasaka, Minato-ku; front & main garden ¥300, palace adult/child/student ¥1500/free/500; ⏰10am-5pm according to opening schedule; 🚃JR lines to Yotsuya)

Zōjō-ji
BUDDHIST TEMPLE

6 ◉ MAP P68, G6

One of the most important temples of the Jōdo (Pure Land) sect of Buddhism, Zōjō-ji dates from 1393 and was the funerary temple of the Tokugawa regime. It's an impressive sight, particularly the main gate, **Sangedatsumon** (三解脱門), constructed in 1605, with its three sections designed to symbolise the three stages one must pass through to achieve nirvana. The **Daibonsho** (Big Bell; 1673) is

Complex 665

This three-storey **building** (Map p68, C5; 6-5-24 Roppongi, Minato-ku; ⏰11am-7pm Tue-Sat; Ⓢ Hibiya line to Roppongi, exit 1) tucked on a backstreet is the shared location of three leading commercial art galleries: **Taka Ishii** (www.takaishiigallery.com), **ShugoArts** (http://shugoarts.com) and **Tomio Koyama Gallery** (www.tomiokoyamagallery.com). The free shows cover a broad spectrum of Japanese contemporary works and are generally worth a look.

a 15-tonne whopper considered one of the great three bells of the Edo period. (増上寺; ☏03-3432-1431; www.zojoji.or.jp/en/index.html; 4-7-35 Shiba-kōen, Minato-ku; admission free; ⏰dawn-dusk; Ⓢ Ōedo line to Daimon, exit A3)

Eating

Sougo
JAPANESE ¥

7 ✖ MAP P68, C4

Sit at the long counter beside the open kitchen or in booths and watch the expert chefs prepare delicious and beautifully presented *shōjin-ryōri* (mainly vegetarian cuisine as served at Buddhist temples – note some dishes use *dashi* stock, which contains fish). Lunch is a bargain. Reserve at least one day in advance if you want a vegan

Tokyo Tower

🔭

Looking fabulous when illuminated at night, **Tokyo Tower** (Map p68, F6; 東京タワー; www.tokyotower.co.jp/en.html; 4-2-8 Shiba-kōen, Minato-ku; adult/child/student main deck ¥900/400/500, incl special deck ¥2800/1200/1800; ⏰observation deck 9am-10.30pm; ⑤Ōedo line to Akabanebashi, Akabanebashi exit) is an iconic sight *and* a shameless tourist trap. This 1958-vintage tower – painted bright orange and white in order to comply with international aviation safety regulations – remains a beloved symbol of the city's post-WWII rebirth. At 333m it's 13m taller than the Eiffel Tower, which was the inspiration for its design. Access to the main observation deck at 150m is anytime, but if you want to go to the top deck (250m) a reservation for an allocated time slot is required.

meal (lunch/dinner ¥7000/10,000) prepared. (宗胡; 📞03-5414-1133; www.sougo.tokyo; 3rd fl, Roppongi Green Bldg, 6-1-8 Roppongi, Minato-ku; set meals lunch/dinner from ¥1500/6500; ⏰11.30am-3pm & 6-11pm Mon-Sat; 🍴; ⑤Hibiya line to Roppongi, exit 3)

Honmura-An
SOBA ¥

8 🍴 MAP P68, C4

This fabled soba shop, once located in Manhattan, now serves its hand-made buckwheat noodles at this rustically contemporary noodle shop on a Roppongi side street. The delicate flavour of these noodles is best appreciated when served on a bamboo mat, with tempura or with dainty slices of *kamo* (duck). (本むら庵; 📞03-5772-6657; www.honmuraantokyo.com; 7-14-18 Roppongi, Minato-ku; noodles from ¥900; set meals lunch/dinner ¥1600/7400; ⏰noon-2.30pm & 5.30-10pm Tue-Sun, closed 1st & 3rd Tue of month; 🛜; ⑤Hibiya line to Roppongi, exit 4)

Gogyō
RAMEN ¥

9 🍴 MAP P68, A5

Keep an eye on the open kitchen: no, that's not your dinner going up in flames but the cooking of *kogashi* (burnt) ramen, which this dark and stylish *izakaya* (Japanese pub-eatery) specialises in. It's the burnt lard that gives the broth its dark and intense flavour. Try the 'special *kogashi miso-men*'; there are lots of other dishes on the menu, too. (五行; 📞03-5775-5566; www.ramendining-gogyo.com; 1-4-36 Nish-Azabu, Minato-ku; ramen ¥890-1290; ⏰11.30am-4pm & 5pm-3am, to midnight Sun; ⑤Hibiya line to Roppongi, exit 2)

Jōmon
IZAKAYA ¥¥

10 🍴 MAP P68, C5

This cosy kitchen has bar seating, rows of ornate *shōchū* (liquor) jugs lining the wall and hundreds of freshly prepared skewers splayed in front of the patrons – don't miss the heavenly *zabuton* beef stick. Jōmon is almost directly across from the Family Mart – look for the name in Japanese on the door. Cover charge ¥300 per person. (ジョウモン; ☏03-3405-2585; www.teyandei.com; 5-9-17 Roppongi, Minato-ku; skewers ¥250-500, dishes from ¥580; ◷5.30-11.45pm Sun-Thu, to 5am Fri & Sat; ⚲; Ⓢ Hibiya line to Roppongi, exit 3)

Kikunoi KAISEKI ¥¥¥

11 🍽 MAP P68, C2

Exquisitely prepared seasonal dishes are as beautiful as they are delicious at this Tokyo outpost of one of Kyoto's most acclaimed *kaiseki* (Japanese haute cuisine) restaurants. Kikunoi's third-generation chef, Murata Yoshihiro, has written a book translated into English on *kaiseki* that the staff helpfully use to explain the dishes you are served, if you don't speak Japanese. (菊乃井; ☏03-3568-6055; www.kikunoi.jp; 6-13-8 Akasaka, Minato-ku; lunch/dinner course from ¥11,900/16,000; ◷noon-12.30pm Tue-Sat, 5-7.30pm Mon-Sat; Ⓢ Chiyoda line to Akasaka, exit 7)

Tofuya-Ukai KAISEKI ¥¥¥

12 🍽 MAP P68, F6

One of Tokyo's most gracious restaurants is located in a former sake brewery (moved from northern Japan), with an exquisite traditional garden, in the shadow of Tokyo Tower. Seasonal preparations of tofu and accompanying dishes are served in the refined *kaiseki* style. Reserve well in advance. Vegetarians should tell the staff when they book. (とうふ屋うかい; ☏03-3436-1028;

Roppongi, Akasaka & Around Eating

Kaiseki at Kikunoi

Pasela Resorts

With decor that is a cut above the other yodelling parlours, **Pasela** (パセラリゾーツ; Map p68, D5; 0120-911-086; www. pasela.co.jp/shop/roppongi/ karaoke; 5-16-3 Roppongi, Minato-ku; per hour per person Sun-Thu ¥1100, Fri & Sat ¥1300; noon-6am Sun-Thu, to 7am Fri & Sat; Hibiya line to Roppongi, exit 3) offers six floors of karaoke rooms (including swanky VIP suites), an extensive selection of Western songs, and wine, champagne and sweets on the menu. The two-hour *nomihōdai* (all-you-can-drink) package (per person ¥3700, ¥4200 on Friday; room rental included) is a good deal.

www.ukai.co.jp/english/shiba; 4-4-13 Shiba-kōen, Minato-ku; set meals lunch/dinner from ¥5940/10,800; 11.45am-3pm & 5-7.30pm Mon-Fri, 11am-7.30pm Sat & Sun; ; Ōedo line to Akabanebashi, exit 8)

Drinking

Gen Yamamoto
COCKTAIL BAR

13 MAP P68, C6

The delicious fruit-based drinks served here use local seasonal ingredients. Yamamoto's tasting menus are designed to be savoured, not to get you sozzled (servings are small), and the bar's ambience – eight seats around a bar

made from 500-year-old Japanese oak – is reminiscent of a traditional teahouse. We highly recommend the six-cocktail menu. (ゲンヤマモト; 03-6434-0652; www.genyama-moto.jp; 1-6-4 Azabu-Jūban, Minato-ku; cover charge ¥1000, 4-/6-cocktail menu ¥4700/6700; 3-11pm Tue-Sun; Namboku line to Azabu-Jūban, exit 7)

Two Dogs Taproom
CRAFT BEER

14 MAP P68, D4

There are 24 taps devoted to Japanese and international craft beers, including its own Roppongi Pale Ale, at this convivial pub just off the main Roppongi drag. Work your way through a few jars to wash down the tasty and decent-sized pizzas. (03-5413-0333; www. twodogs-tokyo.com; 3-15-24 Roppongi, Minato-ku; 11.30am-2.30pm Mon-Fri, 5-11pm Sun & Mon, to midnight Tue & Wed, to 2am Thu-Sat; Hibiya line to Roppongi, exit 3)

Garden
CAFE

15 MAP P68, C6

Stare out from this serene tea lounge across the beautiful late-16th-century garden, hidden behind International House of Japan. There are plenty of tempting pastries and cakes, as well as more substantial meals should you wish to linger – and who could blame you! Tea and coffee from ¥540. (03-3470-4611; www.i-house. or.jp/eng/facilities/tealounge; International House of Japan, 5-11-16 Roppongi, Minato-ku; 7am-10pm; ; Ōedo line to Azabu-Jūban, exit 7)

Shopping

Japan Traditional Crafts Aoyama Square

ARTS & CRAFTS

16 MAP P68, B1

Supported by the Japanese Ministry of Economy, Trade and Industry, this is as much a showroom as a shop, exhibiting a broad range of traditional crafts from around Japan, including lacquerwork boxes, woodwork, cut glass, textiles and pottery. There are some exquisite heirloom pieces here, but also beautiful items at reasonable prices. (伝統工芸青山スクエア; ☎03-5785-1301; www.kougeihin.jp; 8-1-22 Akasaka, Minato-ku; ⏰11am-7pm; Ⓢ Ginza line to Aoyama-itchōme, exit 4)

Tokyo Midtown

MALL

17 MAP P68, C3

This sleek complex, where escalators ascend alongside waterfalls of rock and glass, brims with sophisticated shops. Most notable is the selection of homewares and lifestyle boutiques, including **The Cover Nippon** and **Wise-Wise**, which carry works by Japanese designers and artisans, on the 3rd floor of the Galleria section. (東京ミッドタウン; www.tokyo-midtown.

TK KURIKAWA / SHUTTERSTOCK ©

Tokyo Midtown

com; 9-7 Akasaka, Minato-ku; ⏰11am-9pm; Ⓢ Ōedo line to Roppongi, exit 8)

Axis Building

DESIGN

18 MAP P68, D5

This high-end design complex is filled with galleries and shops selling art books, photographs, covetable homewares and other *objets d'art*. (アクシスビル; www.axisinc.co.jp; 5-17-1 Roppongi, Minato-ku; ⏰most shops 11am-7pm Mon-Sat; Ⓢ Hibiya line to Roppongi, exit 3)

Ebisu, Meguro & Around

This trio of largely residential districts is where Tokyo takes on a more human scale. There are some excellent art museums in Ebisu and Meguro, and trendsetting boutiques in Daikanyama and Naka-Meguro. Ebisu in particular has a dynamic dining and bar scene – worth checking out even if you pass on the sights.

The Short List

○ **TOP Museum (p81)** *View works by icons of Japanese photography and up-and-comers.*

○ **Okura (p79)** *Browse artsy items in this landmark store – typical of the trendy shops found across Daikanyama and Naka-Meguro.*

○ **Gem by Moto (p83)** *Visit the tiny watering hole, one of several jewels in the Ebisu bar scene.*

○ **Beer Museum Yebisu (p81)** *Learn about the history of beer in Japan.*

○ **Tokyo Metropolitan Teien Art Museum (p81)** *Discover the exhibitions of decorative arts hosted by this art deco building.*

Getting There & Around

🚃 The JR Yamanote line stops at Ebisu and Meguro stations. The Tōkyū Tōyoko line runs from Shibuya to Daikanyama and Naka-Meguro; some Fukutoshin subway trains continue on the Tōyoko line.

Ⓢ The Hibiya line stops at Ebisu and Naka-Meguro. The Namboku and Mita lines stop at Meguro and Shirokanedai.

Neighbourhood Map on p80

Cherry blossoms over Meguro-gawa (p79) PICTURE CELLS / SHUTTERSTOCK ©

Walking Tour 🥾

Shopping in Daikanyama & Naka-Meguro

Many Japanese fashion brands – high-fashion and street; established and not (yet) – have boutiques in the neighbouring 'hoods of Daikanyama and Naka-Meguro. Both are great for scouting unique pieces and outside-the-mainstream looks. The pace here is noticeably unhurried, encouraged by outdoor cafes and leafy sidewalks.

Walk Facts

Start Okura;
🚇Daikanyama Station

End Vase; Ⓢ Naka-Meguro Station

Length 1km; one to two hours

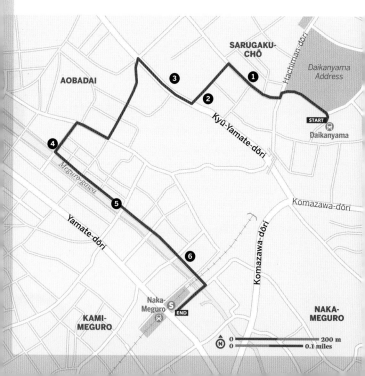

❶ Okura

Okura (オクラ; ☏03-3461-8511; www.hrm.co.jp; 20-11 Sarugaku-chō, Shibuya-ku; ⏱11.30am-8pm Mon-Fri, 11am-8.30pm Sat & Sun) may seem out of place in trendy Daikanyama (the shop looks like a farmhouse), but it is actually a neighbourhood landmark. It's full of artsy original clothing items, almost all of which are made from natural textiles and dyed a deep indigo blue.

❷ Minä Perhonen

Minä Perhonen (☏03-6826-3770; www.mina-perhonen.jp; Daikanyama Hillside Terrace, 18-12 Sarugakuchō, Shibuya-ku; ⏱11am-8pm), from designer Minagawa Akira, is one of Japan's most successful womenswear labels, known for its instantly classic prints in soft, flattering colours; luxurious fabrics; and loose silhouettes that are both sufficiently sophisticated and easy to wear.

❸ Daikanyama T-Site

Locals love **Daikanyama T-Site** (代官山T-SITE; ☏03-3770-2525; http://real.tsite.jp/daikanyama/; 17-5 Sarugaku-chō, Shibuya-ku; ⏱7am-2am). This stylish shrine to the printed word has fantastic books on travel, art, design and food (some in English). You can even sit at the in-house Starbucks and read all afternoon – if you can get a seat.

❹ ...research General Store

...research General Store (www.sett.co.jp; 1-14-11 Aobadai, Meguro-ku; ⏱noon-7pm;) sells original made-in-Japan outdoor wear and gear for the most stylish of mountain hermits (or what designer Kobayashi Setsumasa calls 'anarcho-mountaineers' and 'saunter punks'). There's plenty in here to appeal to the more sedentary, too, like T-shirts and tableware.

❺ Meguro-gawa

It's the **Meguro-gawa** (目黒川), which is not so much a river as a canal, that gives Naka-Meguro it's unlikely village vibe. On either side are walking paths lined with cherry trees – it is a great *hanami* spot – plus shops, restaurants and cafes.

❻ Vase

A perfect example of one of Naka-Meguro's tiny, impeccably curated boutiques, **Vase** (☏03-5458-0337; www.vasenakameguro.com; 1-7-7 Kami-Meguro, Meguro-ku; ⏱noon-8pm) stocks avant-garde designers and vintage pieces. It's in a little white house set back from the Meguro-gawa (the name is on the post box).

Ebisu, Meguro & Around

DŌGENZAKA

Shibuya **S**

Keiō
Shibuya

MARUYAMA-
CHŌ

JR Shibuya

Tōkyū
Shibuya **S**

SAKURAGAOKA-
CHŌ

Shuto Expwy No 3

DAIKANYAMA

Meiji-dōri

3 Yamatane
Museum of Art

SARUGAKU-
CHŌ

Hachiman-dōri

Kyū-Yamate-dōri

HIRO-O

Komazawa-dōri

EBISU-
NISHI

AOBADAI

Daikanyama

Kyū Asakura
House

13

11 ●
Ebisu **S**

6

Ebisu-higashi
kōen

Meiji-dōri

10

Ebisu-
yokochō

EBISU

9

Komazawa-dōri

7

Naka-
Meguro **S**

12

KAMI-
MEGURO

8

EBISU-
MINAMI

NAKA-
MEGURO

14

Ebisu-
minami kōen

Kusunoki-
dōri

4 Beer Museum
Yebisu

Sky Walk

Platanus-
dōri

2 TOP
Museum

Yamate-dōri

Chaya-zaka (slope)

MITA

Shuto Expwy No 2

Institute
for
Nature
Study

Komazawa-dōri

MEGURO-KU

Meguro-dōri

Tokyo Metropolitan ●
Teien Art Museum 1

MEGURO

KAMI-
ŌSAKI

SHINAGAWA-KU

SHIMO-
MEGURO

5

Meguro **S**

Meguro-dōri

For reviews see

●	Sights	p81
✕	Eating	p82
●	Drinking	p83
●	Entertainment	p84
●	Shopping	p85

0 ———— 400 m
0 ———— 0.2 miles

Sights

Tokyo Metropolitan Teien Art Museum
MUSEUM

1 ⊙ MAP P80, D5

Although the Teien museum often hosts excellent exhibitions – usually of decorative arts – its chief appeal lies in the building itself: it's an art deco structure, a former princely estate built in 1933, designed by French architect Henri Rapin, with much of the original interior intact. Tip: budget time to lounge around on the manicured lawn. There is also a modern annex designed by artist Sugimoto Hiroshi. Note that the museum is closed between exhibitions. (東京都庭園美術館; www.teien-art-museum.ne.jp; 5-21-9 Shirokanedai, Minato-ku; adult/child ¥1200/960; ◷10am-6pm, closed 2nd & 4th Wed of each month; 🚊JR Yamanote line to Meguro, east exit)

TOP Museum
MUSEUM

2 ⊙ MAP P80, D4

Tokyo's principal photography museum usually holds three different exhibitions at once, drawing on both its extensive collection of Japanese artists and images on loan. Shows may include the history of photography, retrospectives of major artists or surveys of up-and-coming ones. (東京都写真美術館, Tokyo Photographic Arts Museum; 📞03-3280-0099; www.topmuseum.jp; 1-13-3 Mita, Meguro-ku; ¥500-1000; ◷10am-6pm Tue, Wed, Sat & Sun, to 8pm Thu & Fri; 🚊JR Yamanote line to Ebisu, east exit)

Yamatane Museum of Art
MUSEUM

3 ⊙ MAP P80, D2

When Western ideas entered Japan following the Meiji Restoration (1868), many artists set out to master oil and canvas. Others poured new energy into *nihonga* (Japanese-style painting, typically done with mineral pigments on silk or paper) and that's what is featured here. From the collection of 1800 works, a small number are displayed in thematic exhibitions (some famous works are usually included). Note that the museum is closed between exhibitions. (山種美術館; 📞03-5777-8600; www.yamatane-museum.or.jp; 3-12-36 Hiro-o, Shibuya-ku; adult/student/child ¥1000/800/free, special exhibits extra; ◷10am-5pm Tue-Sun; 🚊JR Yamanote line to Ebisu, west exit)

Beer Museum Yebisu
MUSEUM

4 ⊙ MAP P80, D3

Photos, vintage bottles and posters document the rise of Yebisu, and beer in general, in Japan at this small museum located where the actual Yebisu brewery stood from the late 19th century until 1988. At the 'tasting salon' you can sample four kinds of Yebisu beer (¥400 each or three smaller glasses for ¥800). It's behind the Mitsukoshi department store at

Yebisu Garden Place. (エビスビール記念館; 📞03-5423-7255; www.sapporoholdings.jp/english/guide/yebisu; 4-20-1 Ebisu, Shibuya-ku; admission free; ⏰11am-7pm Tue-Sun; 🚉JR Yamanote line to Ebisu, east exit)

Eating

Tonki

TONKATSU ¥

5  MAP P80, D5

Tonki is a Tokyo *tonkatsu* legend, deep-frying pork cutlets, recipe unchanged, for nearly 80 years. The seats at the counter – where you can watch the perfectly choreographed chefs – are the most coveted, though there is usually a queue. There are tables upstairs. (とんき; 📞03-3491-9928; 1-2-1 Shimo-Meguro, Meguro-ku;

meals ¥1800; ⏰4-10.45pm Wed-Mon, closed 3rd Mon of each month; 🚉JR Yamanote line to Meguro, west exit)

Afuri

RAMEN ¥

6 MAP P80, C3

Afuri has been a major player in the local ramen scene, making a strong case for a light touch with its signature yuzu-shio (a light, salty broth flavoured with yuzu, a type of citrus) ramen. It's since opened branches around the city, but this industrial-chic Ebisu shop is the original. It now does a vegan ramen. Order from the vending machine. (あふり; www.afuri.com; 1-1-7 Ebisu, Shibuya-ku; ramen from ¥980; ⏰11am-5am; v; 🚉JR Yamanote line to Ebisu, east exit)

Kyū Asakura House

Delifucious

BURGERS ¥

7 🍴 MAP P80, A3

What happens when a former Ginza sushi chef turns his attention to – of all things – hamburgers? You get fish burgers and *anago* (conger eel) hot dogs prepared with the same attention to ingredients, preparation and presentation that you'd expect from a high-end sushi counter (but at a far more acceptable price). (📞 03-6874-0412; www.delifucious.com; 1-9-13 Higashiyama, Meguro-ku; burgers from ¥1000; 🕙 noon-9pm Thu-Tue; Ⓢ Hibiya line to Naka-Meguro, main exit)

Yakiniku Champion

BARBECUE ¥¥

8 🍴 MAP P80, C3

Champion is one of Tokyo's best spots for *yakiniku* – literally 'grilled meat' and the Japanese term for Korean barbecue. The menu runs the gamut from sweetbreads to the choicest cuts of grade A5 *wagyū*; there's a diagram of the cuts as well as descriptions. It's very popular; reservations recommended. (焼肉チャンピオン; 📞 03-5768-6922; www.yakiniku-champion.com; 1-2-8 Ebisu, Shibuya-ku; dishes ¥780-3300, course from ¥5600; 🕙 5pm-midnight; 🚃 JR Yamanote line to Ebisu, west exit)

Ippo

IZAKAYA ¥¥

9 🍴 MAP P80, D3

This mellow little *izakaya* (Japanese pub-eatery) specialises in simple pleasures: fish and sake (there's an English sign out front

Kyū Asakura House

🔜

The rare example of early-20th-century villa **architecture** (旧朝倉家住宅, Kyū Asakura-ke Jūtaku; Map p80, B3; 📞 03-3476-1021; 29-20 Sarugaku-chō, Shibuya-ku; adult/child ¥100/50; 🕙 10am-6pm Mar-Oct, to 4pm Nov-Feb; 🚃 Tōkyū Tōyoko line to Daikanyama) is so hidden that many locals don't even know it exists. The home, built in 1919 for the family of a local statesman, includes several large tatami rooms, one Western-style drawing room (the fashion at the time) and a strolling garden with stone lanterns.

that says just that). The friendly chefs speak some English and can help you decide what to have grilled, steamed, simmered or fried; if you can't decide, the ¥2500 set menu is great value. The entrance is up the wooden stairs. (一歩; 📞 03-3445-8418; www.sakanabar-ippo.com; 2nd fl, 1-22-10 Ebisu, Shibuya-ku; cover charge ¥500, dishes ¥450-1700; 🕙 6pm-3am; 🚃 JR Yamanote line to Ebisu, east exit)

Drinking

Gem by Moto

BAR

10 🍺 MAP P80, D3

Tiny Gem has a seriously good selection of interesting sakes from ambitious brewers. Start with one

Ebisu Food Stalls 🍴

Locals love **Ebisu-yokochō** (恵比寿横町; Map p80, C3; www. ebisu-yokocho.com; 1-7-4 Ebisu, Shibuya-ku; dishes ¥500-1500; ⏱5pm-late; 🚉JR Yamanote line to Ebisu, east exit), a retro arcade chock-a-block with food stalls dishing up everything from humble *yaki soba* (fried buckwheat noodles) to decadent *hotate-yaki* (grilled scallops). Seating is on stools; some of the tables are made from repurposed beer crates. It's loud and lively pretty much every night of the week; go early to get a table. Hours and prices vary by shop. The entrance is marked with a rainbow-coloured sign.

of the Gem originals (brewed in collaboration with the bar) – or let owner Chiba-san select one for you. Sake by the glass runs from ¥650 to ¥5000 (but most are on the more reasonable end). Cover charge ¥800; reservations recommended. (ジェムバイモト; 📞03-6455-6998; 1-30-9 Ebisu, Shibuya-ku; ⏱5pm-midnight Tue-Fri, 1-9pm Sat & Sun; 🚉JR Yamanote line to Ebisu, east exit)

Bar Trench   COCKTAIL BAR

11 🚇 MAP P80, C3

One of the pioneers in Tokyo's new cocktail scene, Trench (a suitable name for a bar hidden in a narrow alley) is a tiny place with an air of old-world bohemianism – but that might just be the absinthe talking. The always-changing original tipples are made with infusions, botanicals, herbs and spices. Drinks from ¥1500; cover ¥500. (バートレンチ; 📞03-3780-5291; www.small-axe.net; 1-5-8 Ebisu-nishi, Shibuya-ku; ⏱7pm-2am Mon-Sat, 6pm-1am Sun; 🚉JR Yamanote line to Ebisu, west exit)

Onibus Coffee   COFFEE

12 🚇 MAP P80, A3

Local hotspot Onibus Coffee perfectly nails two of Tokyo's current obsessions: third-wave coffee and restored heritage buildings. The beans here are roasted in-house and the cafe is set in a lightly-renovated former tofu shop. (オニバスコーヒー; 📞03-6412-8683; www.onibuscoffee.com; 2-14-1 Kami-Meguro, Meguro-ku; ⏱9am-6pm; ⓈHibiya line to Naka-Meguro, south exit)

Entertainment

Unit   LIVE MUSIC

13 ⭐ MAP P80, B3

This subterranean club stages live music and DJ-hosted events (sometimes staggered on the same night). The solid line-up includes Japanese indie bands, veterans playing to a smaller crowd and overseas artists making their Japan debut. Unit has high ceilings and an intentionally industrial-cool interior (in addition

Ebisu

to excellent sound), separating it from Tokyo's grungier live-music spots. (ユニット; ☎03-5459-8630; www.unit-tokyo.com; 1-34-17 Ebisu-nishi, Shibuya-ku; ticket ¥2500-5000; ®Tōkyū Tōyoko line to Daikanyama)

Shopping

Kapital   FASHION & ACCESSORIES

14 🔒 MAP P80, C3

Cult brand Kapital is hard to pin down, but perhaps a deconstructed mash-up of the American West and the centuries-old Japanese aesthetic of *boro* (tatty) chic comes close. Almost no two items are alike; most are unisex. The shop itself is like an art installation. The staff, not snobby at all, can point you towards the other two shops nearby. (キャピタル; ☎03-5725-3923; www.kapital.jp; 2-20-2 Ebisu-Minami, Shibuya-ku; ⏰11am-8pm; ®JR Yamanote line to Ebisu, west exit)

Shibuya

Shibuya, the heart of Tokyo's youth culture, hits you over the head with its sheer presence: the continuous flow of people, the glowing video screens and the tangible buzz. All of this is summed up by its top attraction, Shibuya Crossing. It's a neighbourhood that is undergoing a massive transformation, evidenced by developments such as Shibuya Stream.

The Short List

◦ **Shibuya Crossing (p93)** *Experience Japan's busiest intersection.*

◦ **Shibuya Center-gai (p93)** *Wander down the neighbourhood's always lively, neon-lit main drag.*

◦ **Tomigaya (p88)** *Check out the hip hang-outs in this up-and-coming 'un-Shibuya'.*

◦ **Shibuya Stream (p92)** *Walk beside the stream at this commercial complex with an outdoor terrace.*

◦ **d47 Museum (p99)** *Visit a showcase for products from Japan's 47 prefectures.*

Getting There & Around

🚃 The JR Yamanote line stops at Shibuya Station. The Keiō Inokashira line departs from Keiō Shibuya Station for Shinsen, Komaba-Todaimae and Shimo-Kitazawa.

Ⓢ The Ginza, Hanzōmon and Fukutoshin lines stop in Shibuya. The Chiyoda line stops at Yoyogi-kōen (for Tomigaya); some Chiyoda line trains continue on the Odakyū line for Shimo-Kitazawa.

Neighbourhood Map on p90

Shibuya Stream (p92) OSUGI / SHUTTERSTOCK ©

Walking Tour 🥾

Hanging out in Tomigaya

For years Tomigaya, a residential part of what's known as Oku-Shibuya ('deep Shibuya'), was a well-kept secret, but with more and more creative cafes, bistros and boutiques opening, the buzz is too great to contain. Take a break from the brashness of central Shibuya – just 15 minutes away on foot – to see what locals are so excited about.

Walk Facts

Start Little Nap Coffee Stand; [S] Yoyogi-kōen Station, exit 3

End Fuglen Tokyo; [S] Chiyoda line to Yoyogi-kōen, exit 2

Length 1km; one to two hours

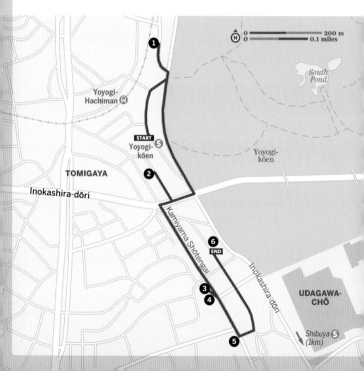

❶ Little Nap Coffee Stand

On the western edge of Yoyogi-kōen, **Little Nap Coffee Stand** (リトルナップコーヒースタンド; www.littlenap.jp; 5-65-4 Yoyogi, Shibuya-ku; ⏰9am-7pm Tue-Sun) is popular with local dog walkers and joggers. The lattes and single-origin pour-overs (¥450; from beans roasted at Little Nap's roaster up the street) are excellent.

❷ Tsukikageya

Natsuki Shigeta designs *yukata* (light cotton kimonos) with a punk-rock slant that pair with wild accessories. Her studio and **shop** (月影屋; www.tsukikageya.com; 1-9-19 Tomigaya, Shibuya-ku; ⏰noon-8pm Thu-Mon, closed irregularly) is tucked away at the back of an apartment complex; enter from the alley behind, and look for the jewellery vending machine out front.

❸ Camelback

Sandwich counter **Camelback** (キャメルバック; www.camelback.tokyo; 42-2 Kamiyama-chō, Shibuya-ku; sandwiches ¥450-900; ⏰8am-5pm Tue-Sun; 🍴) is run by a young and savvy English-speaking crew (among them a trained sushi chef). Get the omelette sandwich, made with the same kind of fluffy, rolled omelette served at sushi restaurants. Seating is on the bench outside.

❹ Archivando

Tiny shop **Archivando** (アルチヴァンド; ☎03-5738-7253; www.archivando.jp; 41-5 Kamiyama-chō, Shibuya-ku; ⏰1-9pm Mon, Tue, Thu & Fri, noon-8pm Sat & Sun) is a convincing example of less is more, featuring minimalist, hand-crafted homewares, clothing and accessories, pop-up shops from obscure artisans and vintage finds.

❺ Shibuya Publishing & Booksellers

Come browse the selection of art, food and travel magazines and small-press offerings at indie bookshop Shibuya Publishing & Booksellers (p99). There's a small selection of books in English, and also other stuff, like totes and accessories from Japanese designers.

❻ Fuglen Tokyo

Fuglen Tokyo (www.fuglen.no; 1-16-11 Tomigaya, Shibuya-ku; ⏰8am-10pm Mon & Tue, to 1am Wed & Thu, to 2am Fri, 9am-2am Sat, 9am-midnight Sun; 📶) – Tomigaya's principal gathering spot – does coffee by day and some of the city's most creative cocktails (from ¥1250) by night (Wednesday to Sunday). Check the calendar for special events, which happen several times a month.

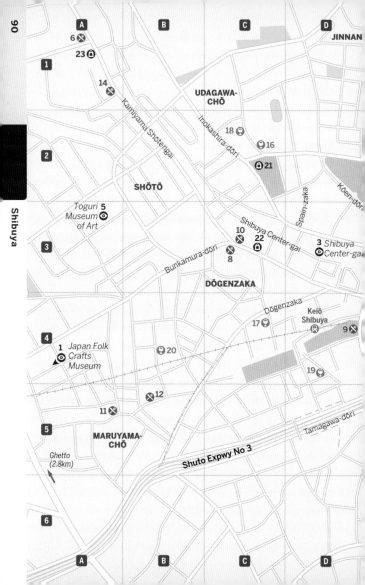

Shibuya

JINNAN

6 ⊗ **A**

23 🔒

14 ⊗

UDAGAWA-CHŌ

Kamiyama Shotengai

Inokashira-dōri

18 🍴

🍴 16

🔒 21

Kōen-dōri

Spain-zaka

SHŌTŌ

Toguri **5**
Museum ◉
of Art

10 ⊗
8

22 🔒

Shibuya Center-gai

3 *Shibuya*
◉ *Center-ga*

Bunkamura-dōri

DŌGENZAKA

Dōgenzaka

17 🍴

Keiō
Shibuya

9 ⊗

1 *Japan Folk*
◢ ◉ *Crafts*
Museum

🍴 20

19 🍴

⊗ 12

11 ⊗

Tamagawa-dōri

5

MARUYAMA-CHŌ

Ghetto
(2.8km)

Shuto Expwy No 3

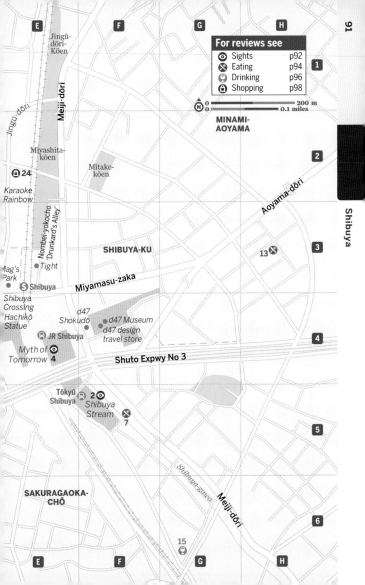

Shibuya

MINAMI-
AOYAMA

For reviews see
- ◉ Sights   p92
- ✕ Eating   p94
- 🅿 Drinking   p96
- 🔒 Shopping   p98

0   200 m
0   0.1 miles

Jingū-
dōri-
Kōen

Miyashita-
kōen

Mitake-
kōen

Karaoke
Rainbow

🔒 24

Nombei-yokocho
'Drunkard's Alley'

● Tight

SHIBUYA-KU

Aoyama-dōri

13 ✕

Mag's
Park

🅂 Shibuya

Miyamasu-zaka

Shibuya
Crossing
Hachikō
Statue

d47
Shokudō

● d47 Museum
d47 design
travel store

🅁 JR Shibuya

Myth of ◉
Tomorrow 4

Shuto Expwy No 3

Tōkyū 🅰 2 ◉
Shibuya   Shibuya
          Stream ✕
          7

Shibuya-gawa

Meiji-dōri

SAKURAGAOKA-
CHŌ

15
🅿

Sights

Japan Folk Crafts Museum

MUSEUM

1 ◎ MAP P90, A4

The *mingei* (folk crafts) movement was launched in the early 20th century to promote the works of artisans over cheaper, mass-produced goods. Central to the *mingei* philosophy is *yo no bi* (beauty through use). The Japan Folk Crafts Museum houses a collection of some 17,000 examples of craftwork from around Japan, in a farmhouse-like building designed by one of the movement's founders. Note that it closes between exhibitions (check the schedule online).

From Komaba-Todaimae Station (two stops from Shibuya on the Keiō Inokashira line), walk with the train tracks on your left; when the road turns right (after about five minutes), the museum will be on your right. (日本民藝館, Mingeikan; http://mingeikan.x0.com; 4-3-33 Komaba, Meguro-ku; adult/student/child ¥1100/600/200; ⏰10am-5pm Tue-Sun; 🚉Keiō Inokashira line to Komaba-Todaimae, west exit)

Shibuya Stream

LANDMARK

2 ◎ MAP P90, F5

It's hard to imagine, but Shibuya Crossing actually sits on the confluence of two rivers: the Shibuya-gawa and the Uda-gawa, which were diverted underground decades ago. Shibuya Stream, part of Shibuya's redevelopment,

Shibuya Center-gai

Shibuya Crossing

Rumoured to be the busiest intersection in the world (and definitely in Japan), **Shibuya Crossing** (Map p90, E4; 渋谷スクランブル交差点, Shibuya Scramble; JR Yamanote line to Shibuya, Hachikō exit) is like a giant beating heart, sending people in all directions with every pulsing light change. Perhaps nowhere else says 'Welcome to Tokyo' better than this. Hundreds of people – and at peak times upwards of 3000 people – cross at a time, coming from all directions at once, yet still managing to dodge each other with a practised, nonchalant agility.

Mag's Park (Map p90, E3; 1-23-10 Jinnan, Shibuya-ku; 11am-11pm; JR Yamanote line to Shibuya, Hachikō exit), the rooftop of the Shibuya 109-2 department store, has the best views over the neighbourhood's famous scramble crossing. It's screened with plexiglass, so you can still get good photos, without having to worry about losing anything over the edge.

The intersection is most impressive after dark on a Friday or Saturday night, when the crowds pouring out of the station are at their thickest and neon-lit by the signs above.

is a step towards bringing the city's waterways back. It's mostly a giant, glass multipurpose complex, but there's a lovely stretch of Shibuya-gawa flanked by terraces and some bars and restaurants. (渋谷ストリーム; https://shibuyastream.jp; 3-21-3 Shibuya, Shibuya-ku; Ginza, Hanzōmon or Fukutoshin line to Shibuya, exit 16b, JR Yamanote line to Shibuya, new south exit)

Shibuya Center-gai   STREET

3 MAP P90, D3

Shibuya's main drag is closed to cars and chock-a-block with fast-food joints and high-street fashion shops. At night, lit bright as day, with a dozen competing soundtracks (coming from who knows where), wares spilling onto the streets and strutting teens, it feels like a block party – or Tokyo's version of a classic Asian night market. (渋谷センター街, Shibuya Sentā-gai; JR Yamanote line to Shibuya, Hachikō exit)

Myth of Tomorrow   PUBLIC ART

4 MAP P90, E4

Okamoto Tarō's mural, *Myth of Tomorrow* (1967), was commissioned by a Mexican luxury hotel but went missing two years later. It finally turned up in 2003 and, in 2008, the haunting 30m-long work, which depicts the atomic bomb exploding over Hiroshima, was installed inside Shibuya Station. It's on the 2nd floor, in the corridor leading to the Inokashira line. (明日の神話, Asu no Shinwa; ☒JR Yamanote line to Shibuya, Hachikō exit)

Toguri Museum of Art   MUSEUM

5 ◉ MAP P90, A3

The Toguri Museum of Art has an excellent collection of Edo-era ceramics, displayed in informative, thematic exhibitions with English explanations – great for getting to know the techniques involved in different styles and the symbolism behind the varied motifs. (戸栗美術館; www.toguri-museum.or.jp; 1-11-3 Shōto, Shibuya-ku; adult/student/child ¥1000/700/400; ⏱10am-5pm Tue-Thu, Sat & Sun, to 8pm Fri; ☒JR Yamanote line to Shibuya, Hachikō exit)

Eating

Uoriki   SEAFOOD ¥

6 ✗ MAP P90, A1

Uoriki is a fishmonger's run by the same family since 1905 (back when Shibuya was practically still a village). There's a restaurant hidden in the back that serves remarkably inexpensive yakizakana teishōku (set meals of grilled fish, rice and miso soup); the house speciality is saba-miso (mackerel simmered in miso). (魚力; ☎03-3476-6709; www.uoriki6709.com; 40-4 Kamiyama-chō, Shibuya-ku; meals from ¥1050; ⏱11am-4pm & 5.30-8.30pm Mon-Sat; Ⓢ Chiyoda line to Yoyogi-kōen, exit 2)

Gyūkatsu Motomura   TONKATSU ¥

7 ✗ MAP P90, F5

You know tonkatsu, the deep-fried breaded pork cutlet that is a Japanese staple; meet gyūkatsu, the deep-fried breaded beef cutlet and much-hyped dish. At Motomura, diners get a small individual grill to cook the meat to their liking. Set meals include cabbage, rice and soup. It's just off Meiji-dōri, at the southern end of Shibuya Stream. (牛かつ もと村; ☎03-3797-3735; www.gyukatsu-motomura.com; basement fl, 3-18-10 Shibuya, Shibuya-ku; set meal from ¥1300; ⏱10am-10pm; ☒JR Yamanote line to Shibuya, east exit)

Sagatani   SOBA ¥

8 ✗ MAP P90, C3

Proving that Tokyo is only expensive to those who don't know better, this all-night joint serves up bamboo steamers of delicious noodles for just ¥320. You won't regret 'splurging' on the ごまだれそば (goma-dare soba; buckwheat noodles with sesame dipping sauce) for ¥450. Look for the stone mill in the window and order from the vending machine. (嵯峨谷; 2-25-7 Dōgenzaka, Shibuya-ku; noodles from ¥320; ⏱24hr; ☒JR Yamanote line to Shibuya, Hachikō exit)

Food Show   SUPERMARKET ¥

9 ✗ MAP P90, D4

A best friend to harried and hungry commuters, Food Show has steamers of dumplings, crisp karaage

Gyūkatsu

(Japanese-style fried chicken), sushi sets and heaps of salads from which to choose, all packaged to go. It's in the basement of Shibuya Station; look for the green signs near Hachikō (the dog statue just outside Shibuya Station) and in the station pointing downstairs. (フードショー; basement fl, 2-24-1 Shibuya, Shibuya-ku; ⏰10am-9pm; 🍴; 🚉JR Yamanote line to Shibuya, Hachikō exit)

Viron
BAKERY ¥

10 ❌ MAP P90, C3

Tokyo's best French bakery (it apparently imports the flour from the motherland) serves up sandwiches and pastries to take away or you can eat them in the cafe upstairs if you want to spring for a drink. (📞03-5458-1770; 33-8 Udagawa-chō, Shibuya-ku; pastries from ¥350, sandwiches ¥650-1300; ⏰9am-10pm; 🍴; 🚉JR Yamanote line to Shibuya, Hachikō exit)

Kaikaya
SEAFOOD ¥¥

11 ❌ MAP P90, A5

Traveller favourite Kaikaya serves seafood, much of which is caught in nearby Sagami Bay, in a variety of styles. The whole casual set-up is a homage to the sea, with surfboards on the wall. The courses are a good deal; for à la carte orders, there's a ¥400 cover charge. Staff speak good English; reservations recommended. (開花屋; 📞03-3770-0878; www.kaikaya.com; 23-7 Maruyama-chō, Shibuya-ku; lunch from ¥850, dishes ¥850-2300, set course from ¥3500; ⏰11.30am-2pm & 5.30-10.30pm Mon-Fri, 5.30-10.30pm Sat & Sun; 🚉JR Yamanote line to Shibuya, Hachikō exit)

Nonbei-yokochō

Nonbei-yokochō – literally 'Drunkard's Alley' – is one of Tokyo's strips of tiny wooden shanty bars, here in the shadow of the elevated JR tracks. Note that some of the bars have cover charges (usually ¥500 to ¥1000). **Tight** (タイト; Map p90, E3; 2nd fl, 1-25-10 Shibuya, Shibuya-ku; ⏰6pm-2am Mon-Sat; 🚉JR Yamanote line to Shibuya, Hachikō exit) is one that doesn't.

Matsukiya   HOTPOT ¥¥¥

12 🍴 MAP P90, B5

There are only two things on the menu at Matsukiya, established in 1890: sukiyaki (thinly sliced beef, simmered and dipped in raw egg) and shabu-shabu (the same meat swished in hot broth and dipped in a citrusy soy sauce or sesame sauce). The beef is top-grade wagyū from Ōmi. Meals include veggies and noodles cooked in the broths. (松木家; 📞03-3461-2651; 6-8 Maruyama-chō, Shibuya-ku; meals from ¥5400; ⏰5-11pm Mon-Sat; 🚉JR Yamanote line to Shibuya, Hachikō exit)

Narukiyo   IZAKAYA ¥¥¥

13 🍴 MAP P90, H3

Cult favourite izakaya (Japanese pub-eatery), Narukiyo serves seasonal Japanese cuisine with creative panache. The menu, which changes daily, is handwritten on a scroll and totally undecipherable; say the magic word, omakase (chef's choice; and set a price cap, say ¥5000 or ¥7000 per person), and trust that you're in good hands. Reservations recommended. (なるきよ; 📞03-5485-2223; 2-7-14 Shibuya, Shibuya-ku; dishes ¥700-4800; ⏰6pm-12.30am; 🚉JR Yamanote line to Shibuya, east exit)

Pignon   BISTRO ¥¥¥

14 🍴 MAP P90, A1

Pignon is a perfect example of where Tokyo's dining scene is going: it's ostensibly a bistro, sources its ingredients directly from producers and has a menu influenced by chef Yoshikawa Rimpei's global travels. In other words, it's laying down local roots, riffing on the classics and chomping on the bit to break free from convention. (ピニョン; 📞03-3468-2331; www.pignontokyo.jp; 16-3 Kamiyama-chō, Shibuya-ku; dishes ¥1700-4200; ⏰6.30-10.30pm Mon-Sat; 🚉JR Yamanote line to Shibuya, Hachikō exit)

Drinking

Circus Tokyo   CLUB

15 🍸 MAP P90, G6

Circus, the Tokyo offshoot of an Osaka club, is aggressively underground: small, out of the way, in a basement (of course), with no decor to speak of and all attention laser-focused on the often experimental music. It's open most Fridays and Saturdays from 11pm, and sometimes other nights; check the schedule. Cover ¥2000 to ¥3000 and drinks ¥600; ID required. (www.circus-tokyo.jp; 3-26-16 Shibuya, Shibuya-ku; 🚉 JR Yamanote line to Shibuya, new south exit)

Gen Gen An TEAHOUSE

16 🚇 MAP P90, C2

Your Shibuya pit stop for green-tea lattes, fresh-brewed ice teas, earthy *hōjicha* (roasted tea) and more, all made from organic leaves harvested in Saga prefecture. (幻幻庵; https://en-tea.com; 4-8 Udagawa-chō, Shibuya-ku; 🕐 11am-7pm Tue, Wed & Sun, to 11pm Thu-Sat; 🚉 JR Yamanote line to Shibuya, Hachikō exit)

Contact CLUB

17 🚇 MAP P90, C4

Shibuya's most fashionable club at the time of research, Contact is several stories under a parking garage. Come after 1am on a Friday or Saturday night to see it in top form. Music may be hip-hop, house or techno – depends on the night. It has plenty of space for just lounging, too. To enter, you must first sign up for a membership. ID required. (コンタクト; 📞 03-6427-8107; www.contacttokyo.com; basement, 2-10-12 Dōgenzaka, Shibuya-ku; 🕐 Fri-Wed; 🚉 JR Yamanote line to Shibuya, Hachikō exit)

Rhythm Cafe BAR

18 🚇 MAP P90, C2

Rhythm Cafe is a fun little spot secreted among the windy streets of Udagawa-chō. It's run by a record label and known for having off-beat event nights, such as the retro Japanese pop night on the fourth Thursday of the month. Drinks start at ¥600; some events have a cover, but not usually more than ¥1000.

Shibuya Drinking

Shimo-Kitazawa

The narrow streets of 'Shimokita', barely passable by cars, create a streetscape like a dollhouse version of Tokyo. It's been a favourite haunt of generations of students, musicians and artists. If hippies – not bureaucrats – ran Tokyo, the city would look a lot more like Shimo-Kitazawa. Unfortunately, the massive redevelopment of the train station area is cramping its style a bit, but it's still a great place to wander – and bar-hop. One of the neighbourhood's top bars is **Ghetto** (月灯; Map p90, A5; 1-45-16 Daizawa, Setagaya-ku; 🕐 8.30pm-late; 🚉 Keiō Inokashira line to Shimo-Kitazawa, north exit), inside the iconic (and rickety) Suzunari theatre complex.

Restaurants, bars and entertainment venues are clustered on the south side; the more laid-back north side has many cafes and secondhand shops.

Karaoke Rainbow

This is Shibuya's most popular **karaoke spot** (Map p90, E2; ☏03-6455-3240; www.karaoke-rainbow.com; 8th fl, Shibuya Modi, 1-21-3 Shibuya, Shibuya-ku; per 30min before/after 7pm ¥150/410; ☉11am-5am; ℝJR Yamanote line to Shibuya, Hachikō exit) for two reasons: it doesn't have the same dated look as the generic chains and you get the first hour free (though technically you need to buy one drink; from ¥465). Staff speak some English and the English song list is extensive. It's on the 8th floor of the building with the Marui department store.

(リズムカフェ; ☏03-3770-0244; http://rhythmcafe.jp; 11-1 Udagawa-chō, Shibuya-ku; ☉6pm-2am; ℝJR Yamanote line to Shibuya, Hachikō exit)

Oath   BAR

19 🚇 MAP P90, D4

Oath is a tiny space covered in gilt and mirrors, dripping in chandeliers and absolutely not taking itself seriously. It's a very popular spot for prepartying and afterpartying, thanks to cheap drinks (¥500), fun DJs and a friendly crowd. Cover charge is ¥1000 with one drink included. (www.djbar-oath.com; basement fl, 1-6-5 Dōgenzaka, Shibuya-ku; ☉8pm-5am Mon-Sat; ℝJR Yamanote line to Shibuya, Hachikō exit)

Womb   CLUB

20 🚇 MAP P90, B4

A long-time (in club years, at least) club-scene fixture, Womb is a reliable good night out on a Friday or Saturday if you want to lose yourself in the music (mostly house and techno) and the club's famous laser light shows. Weekdays are hit or miss. Cover ¥1500 to ¥4000; ID required. (ウーム; ☏03-5459-0039, VIP reservations 050-3188-9608; www.womb.co.jp; 2-16 Maruyama-chō, Shibuya-ku; ☉11pm-4.30am Fri & Sat, from 10pm Mon-Thu, varies Sun; ℝJR Yamanote line to Shibuya, Hachikō exit)

Shopping

Tokyu Hands   DEPARTMENT STORE

21 🔒 MAP P90, C2

This DIY and *zakka* (miscellaneous things) store has eight fascinating floors of everything you didn't know you needed – reflexology slippers, bee-venom face masks and cartoon-character-shaped rice-ball moulds, for example. Most stuff is inexpensive, making it perfect for souvenir- and gift-hunting. Warning: you could lose hours in here. (東急ハンズ; http://shibuya.tokyu-hands.co.jp; 12-18 Udagawa-chō, Shibuya-ku; ☉10am-9pm; ℝJR Yamanote line to Shibuya, Hachikō exit)

Mega Donki   VARIETY

22 🔒 MAP P90, C3

You could show up in Tokyo completely empty-handed and

d47 Museum, Travel Store & Cafe

Lifestyle brand D&Department combs the country for the platonic ideals of the utterly ordinary: the perfect broom, bottle opener or salt shaker (to name a few examples). See rotating exhibitions of its latest finds from all 47 prefectures at this one-room **museum** (Map p90, F4; www.hikarie8.com; 8th fl, Shibuya Hikarie, 2-21-1 Shibuya, Shibuya-ku; admission free; ⏱11am-8pm).

The excellent **d47 design travel store** (Map p90, F4; ☏03-6427-2301; ⏱11am-8pm) is next door while the cafe **d47 Shokudō** (d47 食堂; Map p90, F4; meals ¥1550-1780; ⏱11.30am-2.30pm & 6-10.30pm) serves a changing line-up of *teishoku* (set meals) that evoke the specialities of each prefecture, from the fermented tofu of Okinawa to the stuffed squid of Hokkaidō.

his huge outpost of all-night, argain retailer 'Don Quijote' vould have you covered. There re groceries, toiletries, electronics and clothes – along with all orts of random stuff, including he best selection of unusual-lavoured Kit-Kat chocolates ve've seen. Don't miss the giant noray eel in the tank at the entrance. (MEGA ドンキ; ☏03-5428-086; 28-6 Udagawa-chō, Shibuya-ku; ⏱24hr; 🚉JR Yamanote line to hibuya, Hachikō exit)

Shibuya Publishing Booksellers

BOOKS

3 🔒 MAP P90, A1

his indie bookshop, open late mong the bars of Shibuya's Kamiyamachō *shōtengai* (market treet) offers a selection of art, ood and travel magazines and

small-press offerings. You can also find some books in English, plus totes and other accessories from Japanese designers. (SPBS; ☏03-5465-0588; www.shibuyabooks.co.jp; 17-3 Kamiyamachō, Shibuya-ku; ⏱11am-11pm Mon-Sat, to 10pm Sun; 🚉JR Yamanote line to Shibuya, Hachikō exit)

Tower Records

MUSIC

24 🔒 MAP P90, E2

Yes, Tower lives – in Japan at least! This eight-storey temple of music has a deep collection of Japanese and world music. Even if you're not into buying, it can be a great place to browse and discover local artists. There are lots of listening stations. (タワーレコード; ☏03-3496-3661; http://tower.jp/store/Shibuya; 1-22-14 Jinnan, Shibuya-ku; ⏱10am-11pm; 🚉JR Yamanote line to Shibuya, Hachikō exit)

Explore ◉

Harajuku & Aoyama

Harajuku is one of Tokyo's biggest draws thanks to its grand shrine, Meiji-jingū. It's also a world-renowned fashion shopping destination where the ultra-chic come to browse and be seen. Many boutiques here have been designed by influential architects – another draw. Neighbouring Aoyama is a shopping and dining district for the city's fashionable elite.

The Short List

○ **Meiji-jingū (p102)** Follow the wooded, gravel path to Tokyo's most impressive Shintō shrine.

○ **Omote-sandō (p104)** Take in contemporary architecture and eyebrow-raising consumerism along this wide, boutique-lined boulevard.

○ **Yoyogi-kōen (p107)** Relax in the city's most popular park, which buzzes with life on weekends.

○ **Nezu Museum (p107)** Enjoy the calm galleries and gardens of this excellent antiquities museum.

○ **Farmer's Market@UNU (p110)** Experience a market that's as much a social event as a shopping stop.

Getting There & Around

It's an easy walk between Shibuya and Harajuku.

🚃 The JR Yamanote line stops at Harajuku Station.

Ⓢ Meiji-jingūmae (Chiyoda and Fukutoshin lines) Station is at the Harajuku end of Omote-sandō, and Omote-sandō (Chiyoda, Ginza and Hanzōmon lines) Station, is at the Aoyama end. Gaienmae station is on the Ginza line.

Neighbourhood Map on p106

Tokyu Plaza (p105) JIRAT TEPARAKSA / SHUTTERSTOCK ©

Top Experience 📷

Leave the city behind at Meiji-jingū

Tokyo's grandest Shintō shrine is dedicated to the Emperor Meiji and Empress Shōken, whose reign (1868–1912) coincided with Japan's transformation from isolationist, feudal state to modern nation. Constructed in 1920, the shrine was destroyed in WWII air raids and rebuilt in 1958; however, unlike so many of Japan's postwar reconstructions, Meiji-jingū (明治神宮) has atmosphere in spades.

◎ MAP P106, A2

www.meijijingu.or.jp

1-1 Yoyogi Kamizono-chō, Shibuya-ku

admission free

🕐 dawn–dusk

🚃 JR Yamanote line to Harajuku, Omote-sandō exit

The Gates

The shrine is secreted in a wooded grove, accessed via a long, winding gravel path. At the entrance you'll pass through the first of several towering, wooden *torii* (gates). These mark the boundary between the mundane world and the sacred one; as such, it's the custom to bow upon passing through a *torii*.

The Font

In front of the final *torii* before the main shrine is the *temizuya* (font), where visitors purify themselves by pouring water over their hands (purity is a tenet of Shintoism). To do so, dip the ladle in the water and first rinse your left hand then your right. Pour some water into your left hand and rinse your mouth, then rinse your left hand again. Make sure none of this water gets back into the font!

Main Shrine

The main shrine is built of unpainted cypress wood and has a copper-plated roof. To make an offering here (and, if you like, a wish), toss a coin – a ¥5 coin is considered lucky – into the box, bow twice, clap your hands twice and then bow again. To the right, you'll see kiosks selling *ema* (wooden plaques on which prayers are written) and *omamori* (charms). Our personal favourite is the charm for safe travel, naturally.

Meiji-jingū Gyoen

The shrine itself occupies only a small fraction of the sprawling forested grounds, which contain some 120,000 trees donated from all over Japan. Of this, only the strolling garden **Meiji-jingū Gyoen** (明治神宮御苑, Inner Garden; ¥500; ⏰9am-4.30pm, to 4pm Nov-Feb; 🚇JR Yamanote line to Harajuku, Omote-sandō exit) is accessible to the public. Here there are peaceful walks, a good dose of privacy at weekdays, and spectacular irises in June. The entrance is halfway along the gravel path to the shrine.

★ Top Tips

○ Time your visit for 8am or 2pm to catch the twice-daily ceremonial offering of food and prayers to the gods.

○ Other ceremonies and events happen throughout the year; check the website for a schedule.

✕ Take a Break

Coffee shop **Mori no Terrace** (杜のテラス; 📞03-3379-9222; 1-1 Yoyogi Kamizono-chō, Shibuya-ku; coffee & tea from ¥400; ⏰9am-dusk) is right on the gravel path leading into the shrine grounds.

Walking Tour 🚶

Omote-sandō Architecture

Omote-sandō (表参道), the boulevard that connects Harajuku and Aoyama, is like a walk-through showroom featuring the who's who of striking contemporary buildings, designed by some of the biggest names in Japanese architecture. There's no better (or more convenient) place to gain an overview of Japan's current sense of design.

Walk Facts

Start Tokyu Plaza; S Ginza line to Omote-sandō, exits A3 & B4, 🚃 JR Yamanote line to Harajuku, Omote-sandō exit

End SunnyHills; S Omote-sandō, exit 4

Length 1.2km; one hour

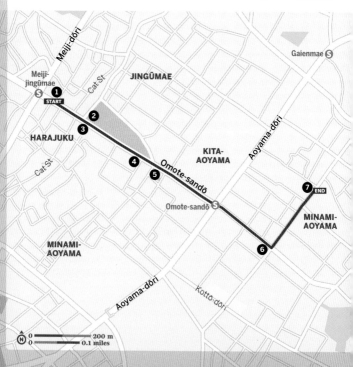

❶ Tokyu Plaza

At the intersection of Omote-sandō and Meiji-dōri stands **Tokyu Plaza** (東急プラザ; 4-30-3 Jingūmae, Shibuya-ku), a castle-like structure built in 2012 and designed by up-and-coming architect Nakamura Hiroshi. The entrance is a dizzying hall of mirrors and there's a roof garden (with a Starbucks) on top.

❷ Omotesandō Hills

Built in 2003, Tadao Ando's **Omotesandō Hills** (表参道ヒルズ; 4-12-10 Jingūmae, Shibuya-ku), is a high-end shopping mall that spirals around a sunken central atrium. Ando's architecture utilises materials such as concrete to create strong geometric shapes, often drawn from Japan's traditional architecture.

❸ Dior Building

Across the street, the five-storey glass **Dior Building** (5-9-11 Jingūmae, Shibuya-ku), designed by SANAA (Nishizawa Ryue and Sejima Kazuyo), has a filmy surface that seems to hang like a dress (an effect achieved with clever lighting and acrylic screens).

❹ Louis Vuitton Building

A couple of blocks down, Aoki Jun's **Louis Vuitton Building** (5-7-5 Jingūmae, Shibuya-ku) has offset panels of tinted glass behind sheets of metal mesh that are meant to evoke a stack of trunks. There's an art gallery on the 7th floor.

❺ Tod's

Climb onto the elevated crosswalk to better admire Ito Toyo's construction for **Tod's** (5-1-15 Jingūmae, Shibuya-ku) . The criss-crossing strips of concrete take their inspiration from the zelkova trees below; they're also structural.

❻ Prada Aoyama Building

You can't miss the **Prada Aoyama Building** (5-2-6 Minami-Aoyama, Minato-ku) with its curvaceous exterior of convex glass bubbles. Created by Herzog & de Meuron, this is the building that escalated the design race in the neighbourhood.

❼ SunnyHills

Turn the corner to see Kengo Kuma's design for Taiwanese pineapple cake shop **SunnyHills** (3-10-20 Minami-Aoyama, Minato-ku). Kuma is an architect known for his use of wood and traditional Japanese joinery techniques, and this building represents his work at its most playful. The 3D-modelled latticework is supposed to evoke a bamboo basket, but also resembles a cross-hatched pineapple.

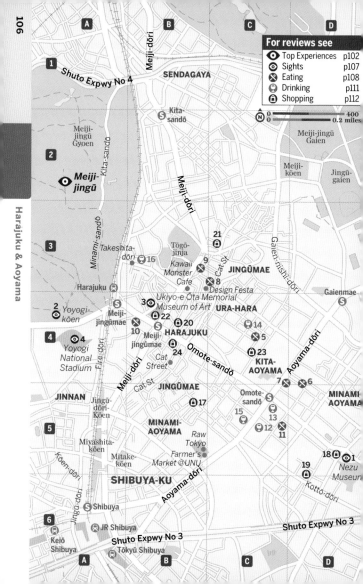

For reviews see

◉ Top Experiences p102
◉ Sights p107
✖ Eating p108
🍷 Drinking p111
🛍 Shopping p112

SENDAGAYA

Kita-sandō

Meiji-jingū Gyoen

◉ Meiji-jingū

Meiji-jingū Gaien

Meiji-kōen

Jingū-gaien

Kita-sandō

Minami-sandō

Takeshita-dōri

Tōgō-jinja

Kawaii Monster Cafe

21

9

Cat St

JINGŪMAE

Harajuku

8

Design Festa

Gaienmae

2 Yoyogi-kōen

3 ◉

Ukiyo-e Ōta Memorial Museum of Art

URA-HARA

22

20

14

5

4 Yoyogi National Stadium

10 Meiji-jingūmae

HARAJUKU

23 KITA-AOYAMA

Cat Street

24

Omote-sandō

JINNAN

Jingū-dōri-Kōen

Cat St

JINGŪMAE

17

7

6

Aoyama-dōri

MINAMI-AOYAMA

Miyashita-kōen

MINAMI-AOYAMA

Omote-sandō

15

13

12 11

SHIBUYA-KU

Raw Tokyo Farmer's Market @UNU

Mitake-kōen

18 ◉ 1 Nezu Museum

19

Kotto-dōri

Kōen-dōri

Aoyama-dōri

Jingu-dōri

Shibuya

6

Keiō Shibuya

JR Shibuya

Shuto Expwy No 3

Tōkyū Shibuya

Shuto Expwy No 3

Shuto Expwy No 4

Meiji-dōri

Meiji-dōri

Meiji-dōri

Gaien-nishi-dōri

Sights

Nezu Museum   MUSEUM

1 ◎ MAP P106, D5

The Nezu Museum offers a striking blend of old and new: a renowned collection of Japanese, Chinese and Korean antiquities in a gallery space designed by contemporary architect Kuma Kengo. Select items from the extensive collection are displayed in seasonal exhibitions. The English explanations are usually pretty good. Behind the galleries is a woodsy strolling garden laced with stone paths and studded with teahouses and sculptures. (根津美術館; ☎03-3400-2536; www.nezu-muse.or.jp; 6-5-1 Minami-Aoyama, Minato-ku; adult/child ¥1100/free, special exhibitions extra ¥200; ⊙10am-5pm Tue-Sun; ⑤Ginza line to Omote-sandō, exit A5)

Yoyogi-kōen   PARK

2 ◎ MAP P106, A4

If it's a sunny and warm weekend afternoon, you can count on there being a crowd lazing around the large grassy expanse that is Yoyogi-kōen. You can also usually find revellers and noisemakers of all stripes, from hula-hoopers to African drum circles to a group of retro greasers dancing around a boom box. It's an excellent park for a picnic and probably the only place in the city where you can reasonably toss a Frisbee without fear of hitting someone. (代々木公園; www.yoyogipark.info; Yoyogi-kamizono-chō, Shibuya-ku; ☒JR Yamanote line to Harajuku, Omote-sandō exit)

Ukiyo-e Ōta Memorial Museum of Art   MUSEUM

3 ◎ MAP P106, B4

This small museum (where you swap your shoes for slippers) is the best place in Tokyo to see *ukiyo-e* (woodblock prints). Each month it presents a seasonal, thematic exhibition (with English curation notes), drawing from the truly impressive collection of Ōta Seizo, the former head of the Toho Life Insurance Company. Most exhibitions include a few works by masters such as Hokusai and Hiroshige. The museum closes the last few days of the month (between exhibitions). (浮世絵太田記念美術館; ☎03-3403-0880; www.ukiyoe-ota-muse.jp; 1-10-10 Jingūmae, Shibuya-ku; adult ¥700-1000, child free; ⊙10.30am-5.30pm Tue-Sun; ☒JR Yamanote line to Harajuku, Omote-sandō exit)

Yoyogi National Stadium   ARCHITECTURE

4 ◎ MAP P106, A4

This early masterpiece by architect Tange Kenzō was built for the 1964 Olympics (and was used again in the 2021 games for the handball event). The stadium, which looks vaguely like a samurai helmet, uses suspension-bridge technology – rather than beams – to support the roof. (国立代々木競技場, Kokuritsu Yoyogi Kyōgi-jō; 2-1-1 Jinnan, Shibuya-ku; ☒JR Yamanote line to Harajuku, Omote-sandō exit)

Kawaii Harajuku

Harajuku is known for its *kawaii* (super cute) fashions and styling. To get an idea of what this is all about, take a look at the shops lining **Takeshita-dōri** (竹下通り; Map p106, B3; Jingūmae, Shibuya-ku; 🚇 JR Yamanote line to Harajuku, Takeshita exit), a pilgrimage site for teens from all over Japan, which means it can get packed. It's an oddly mixed bag: newer shops selling trendy, youthful styles alongside stores still invested in the trappings of decades of subcultures past.

Also check out the darkly cute **Kawaii Monster Cafe** (Map p106, B3; 🕿03-5413-6142; http://kawaiimonster.jp; 4th fl, YM Bldg, 4-31-10 Jingūmae, Shibuya-ku; cover charge ¥500; 🕚11.30am-4.30pm & 6-10.30pm Mon-Sat, 11am-8pm Sun; 🚇JR Yamanote line to Harajuku, Omote-sandō exit), the project of artist and stylist Sebastian Masuda. In the afternoons there's a minimum order of a meal set (from ¥2160, drink included); the photo-ready food is coloured to match the decor. In the evenings the cafe stages various events, which have their own pricing schemes; check ahead before heading out.

Eating

Maisen   TONKATSU ¥

5 🍴 MAP P106, C4

Maison is famous for its *tonkatsu* (breaded, deep-fried pork cutlets) and its setting (an old public bathhouse). There are different grades of pork on the menu, including prized *kurobuta* (black pig), but even the cheapest is melt-in-your-mouth divine; the very reasonable lunch set is served until 4pm. (まい泉; 🕿0120-428-485; www.mai-sen.com; 4-8-5 Jingūmae, Shibuya-ku; lunch/dinner from ¥990/1580; 🕚11am-10.45pm; 👪; 🚇Ginza line to Omote-sandō, exit A2)

Aoyama Kawakami-an   SOBA ¥

6 🍴 MAP P106, D4

This Aoyama outpost of famed Karuizawa soba shop serves handmade, 100% buckwheat noodles all day and (nearly) all night. Go for broke with the (truly) jumbo tempura prawns or add on sides of Nagano specialities like *kurakake mame* (a kind of soy bean) and pickles made of *nozawana* (a kind of mustard leaf). (青山川上庵; 🕿03-5411-7171; 3-14-1 Minami-Aoyama, Minato-ku; soba ¥920-1750; 🕚11.30am-4am; 🚇Ginza line to Omote-sandō, exit A5)

Commune 2nd   MARKET ¥

7 🍴 MAP P106, C4

Commune 2nd is a collection of vendors offering inexpensive

curries, hot dogs, beer and more. Purchase what you want from any of the stalls, then grab a seat at one of the shared picnic tables – this is one of Tokyo's rare al fresco dining spots. It's very popular, especially on a warm Friday or Saturday night. (www.commune2nd.com; 3-13 Minami-Aoyama, Minato-ku; meals ¥1000-1500; ⊘11am-10pm; ⑤Ginza line to Omote-sandō, exit A4)

Sakura-tei OKONOMIYAKI ¥

8 🍴 MAP P106, B3

Grill your own *okonomiyaki* (savoury pancakes) at this funky place inside the gallery **Design Festa** (デザインフェスタ; ☎03-3479-1442; www.designfestagallery.com; 3-20-2 Jingūmae, Shibuya-ku; admission free; ⊘11am-8pm). In addition to classic options (with pork, squid and cabbage), there are some fun fusion-style ones. There's also a great-value, two-hour, all-you-can-eat plan (¥2500 plus one drink order). (さくら亭; ☎03-3479-0039; www.sakuratei.co.jp; 3-20-1 Jingūmae, Shibuya-ku; okonomiyaki ¥1050-1500; ⊘11am-midnight; 🛜🥢; 🚃JR Yamanote line to Harajuku, Takeshita exit)

Agaru Sagaru Nishi-iru Higashi-iru JAPANESE ¥¥

9 🍴 MAP P106, B3

This chill little restaurant serves Kyoto-style food (deceptively simple, with the ingredients – always seasonal – taking centre stage) without pretence. The five-dish course (¥3500) – presented in succession and prettily plated – is perfect for when you want to indulge,

Okonomiyaki

Harajuku & Aoyama Eating

Farmer's Market@UNU

Tokyo's best **farmer's market** (Map p106, B5; www.farmersmarkets.jp; 5-53-7 Jingūmae, Shibuya-ku; ⏱10am-4pm Sat & Sun; Ⓢ Ginza line to Omote-sandō, exit B2) – with colourful produce, pickles and preserves – sets up every weekend on the plaza in front of the United Nations University on Aoyama-dōri. There are always at least half a dozen food trucks here and the market is as much a social event as a shopping stop.

Events pop up, too, including the monthly hipster flea market **Raw Tokyo** (Map p106, B5; www.rawtokyo.jp; 5-53-7 Jingūmae, Shibuya-ku; ⏱11am-5pm 1st weekend of each month; Ⓢ Ginza line to Omote-sandō, exit B2) and the annual **Tokyo Coffee Festival** (https://tokyocoffee festival.co/coffee) and the twice-annual **Aoyama Sake Flea** (www.facebook.com/sakeflea). Check the websites for info on these and other events.

but not too much. (The seven-dish course requires advance reservations.) Also, it looks like a cave. (上下西東; ☎03-3403-6968; basement fl, 3-25-8 Jingūmae, Shibuya-ku; small plates ¥500-900, dinner course ¥3500-5000; ⏱5.30-11.30pm Tue-Sun; Ⓡ JR Yamanote line to Harajuku, Takeshita exit)

Eatrip

BISTRO ¥¥¥

10 🍴 MAP P106, B4

Eatrip is one of the big players in Tokyo's farm-to-table organic movement. Working with domestic food producers, it serves up neo-bistro-style dishes that reflect head chef Shiraishi Takayuki's global travels. Sample dish: *mahata* (grouper; from Mie Prefecture) sautéed with harissa (made in-house), squid ink and *daikon* (radish). Course menu only; reserve ahead. (☎03-3409-4002; www.restaurant-eatrip.com; 6-31-10 Jingūmae, Shibuya-ku; course ¥5400-8640; ⏱6pm-

midnight Tue-Sat, 11.30am-3pm Sat, 11.30am-5pm Sun; Ⓡ JR Yamanote line to Harajuku, Omote-sandō exit)

Yanmo

SEAFOOD ¥¥¥

11 🍴 MAP P106, C5

Freshly caught seafood from the nearby Izu Peninsula is the speciality at this upscale, yet unpretentious restaurant. The dinner courses, which include fish served as sashimi, steamed and grilled, are reasonably priced for what you get; reservations essential. The weekday grilled fish lunch set (¥1200 to ¥1500; chosen from one of several seasonal options) is a bargain; there's usually a queue. (やんも; ☎03-5466-0636; www.yanmo.co.jp/aoyama/index.html; basement fl, T Place bldg, 5-5-25 Minami-Aoyama, Minato-ku; lunch/dinner set menu from ¥1200/7560; ⏱11.30am-2pm & 5.30-10.30pm Mon-Sat; Ⓢ Ginza line to Omote-sandō, exit A5)

Drinking

Sakurai Japanese Tea Experience

TEAHOUSE

12 🚇 MAP P106, C5

Tea master (and former bartender) Sakurai Shinya's contemporary take on the tea ceremony is a must for anyone hoping to be better acquainted with Japan's signature brew. The course includes several varieties – you might be surprised how different tea can taste – paired with small bites, including some beautiful traditional sweets. Come in the evening for tea cocktails. Reservations recommended. (櫻井 焙茶研究所; ☑03-6451-1539; www.sakurai-tea.jp; 5th fl, Spiral Bldg, 5-6-23 Minami-Aoyama, Minato-ku; tea from ¥1400, course from ¥4800; ⏱11am-11pm; Ⓢ Ginza line to Omote-sandō, exit B1)

Aoyama Flower Market Teahouse

TEAHOUSE

13 🚇 MAP P106, C5

Secreted in the back of a flower shop is this fairy-tale teahouse with flower beds running under the glass-top tables and more overhead, plus cut blooms in vases on every available surface. Tea comes by the pot and starts at ¥750; there are pretty sweets and salad spreads on the menu, too. Reservations aren't accepted so you may have to queue. (☑03-3400-0887; www.afm-teahouse.com; 5-1-2 Minami-Aoyama, Minato-ku; ⏱11am-8pm Mon-Sat, to 7pm Sun; Ⓢ Ginza line to Omote-sandō, exit A5)

Koffee Mameya

COFFEE

14 🚇 MAP P106, C4

At any given time, Koffee Mameya has 15 to 20 different beans on rotation from indie roasters around Japan (and some from overseas). Get a cup brewed on the spot or purchase beans for home use; English-speaking baristas can help you narrow down the selection. There's no seating, but you can loiter at the counter. (コーヒーマメヤ; www.koffee-mameya.com; 4-15-3 Jingūmae, Shibuya-ku; coffee ¥350-1100; ⏱10am-6pm; Ⓢ Ginza line to Omote-sandō, exit A2)

Two Rooms

BAR

15 🚇 MAP P106, C5

Expect a crowd dressed like they don't care that wine by the glass starts at ¥1600. You can eat here too, but the real scene is at night by the bar. The terrace has sweeping views towards the Shinjuku skyline. Call ahead (staff speak English) on Friday or Saturday night to reserve a spot under the stars. (トゥールームス; ☑03-3498-0002; www.tworooms.jp; 5th fl, AO Bldg, 3-11-7 Kita-Aoyama, Minato-ku; ⏱11.30am-2am Mon-Sat, to 10pm Sun; Ⓢ Ginza line to Omote-sandō, exit B2)

Harajuku Taproom

PUB

16 🚇 MAP P106, B3

Baird's Brewery is one of Japan's most successful and consistently good craft breweries. This is one of three Tokyo outposts, and you can sample more than a dozen of its beers on tap, including the brewery's Harajuku Real Ale (pints ¥1100). *Yakitori* (grilled chicken skewers) and Japanese pub-style dishes are served as well. (原宿タップルーム; ☑03-6438-0450; https://bairdbeer.com/taprooms/harajuku; 2nd fl, 1-20-13 Jingūmae, Shibuya-ku; ☻5pm-midnight Mon-Fri, noon-midnight Sat & Sun; ☒JR Yamanote line to Harajuku, Takeshita exit)

Shopping

House @Mikiri Hassin FASHION & ACCESSORIES

17 🔒 MAP P106, B5

Hidden deep in Ura-Hara (Harajuku's backstreet area), House stocks an ever-changing selection of experimental Japanese fashion brands. Contrary to what the cool merch might suggest, the sales clerks are polite and friendly – grateful, perhaps, that you made the effort to find the place. Look for 'ハウス' spelled vertically in neon. (ハウス@ミキリハッシン; ☑03-3486-7673; http://house.mikiri-hassin.co.jp; 5-42-1 Jingūmae, Shibuya-ku; ☻noon-9pm Thu-Tue; ☒Ginza line to Omote-sandō, exit A1)

Arts & Science FASHION & ACCESSORIES

18 🔒 MAP P106, D5

Strung along the 1st floor of a mid-century apartment (across from the Nezu Museum) is a collection of small boutiques from celebrity stylist Sonya Park. Park's signature style is a vintage-inspired minimalism in luxurious, natural fabrics. Homewares, too. (www.arts-science.com; 103, 105 & 109 Palace Aoyama, 6-1-6 Minami-Aoyama, Minato-ku; ☻noon-8pm; ☒Ginza line to Omote-sandō, exit A5)

Sou-Sou FASHION & ACCESSORIES

19 🔒 MAP P106, D5

Kyoto brand Sou-Sou is best known for producing the steel-toed, rubber-soled *tabi* shoes worn by Japanese construction workers in fun, playful designs – but they also have clothing and accessories that riff on traditional styles (including some really adorable stuff for kids). (そうそう; ☑03-3407-7877; http://sousou netshop.jp; 5-3-10 Minami-Aoyama, Minato-ku; ☻11am-8pm; ☒Ginza line to Omote-sandō, exit A5)

6% Doki Doki FASHION & ACCESSORIES

20 🔒 MAP P106, B4

Tucked away on an Ura-Hara backstreet, this bubblegum-pink store sells acid-bright accessories that are part raver, part schoolgirl and, according to the store's name, 'six per cent exciting'. We wonder what more excitement would look like! Anyway, it's 100% Harajuku. (ロクパーセントドキドキ; www.dokidoki6.com; 2nd fl, 4-28-16 Jingūmae, Shibuya-ku; ☻noon-8pm; ☒JR Yamanote line to Harajuku, Omote-sandō exit)

Cat Street & Ura-Hara

Had enough of the Harajuku crowds? Exit, stage right, for **Cat Street** (キャットストリート; Map p106, B4; ⏚ JR Yamanote line to Harajuku, Omote-sandō exit), a meandering car-free road with a mishmash of boutiques and a little more breathing room.

Also a little less crowded is Ura-Hara (literally 'the back of Harajuku'), the nickname for the maze of backstreets behind Omotesandō Hills. Here you'll find the ever-changing tiny boutiques and secondhand stores from which Harajuku hipsters cobble together their head-turning looks. Ramshackle art complex Design Festa (p109) is here too, and is a good place to start your explorations.

Musubi   ARTS & CRAFTS

21 MAP P106, C3

Furoshiki are versatile squares of cloth that can be folded and knotted to make shopping bags and gift wrap. This shop sells pretty ones in both traditional and contemporary patterns – sometimes in collaboration with fashion brands. There is usually an English-speaking clerk who can show you some different ways to tie them. (むす美; ☏03-5414-5678; http://kyoto-musubi.com; 2-31-8 Jingūmae, Shibuya-ku; ⏱11am-7pm Thu-Tue; ⏚ JR Yamanote line to Harajuku, Takeshita exit)

Laforet   DEPARTMENT STORE

22 MAP P106, B4

Laforet has been a beacon of Harajuku fashion for decades. Check out the avant-garde looks at ground-floor boutiques **Wall** and **Hoyajuku**; more mainstream boutiques are on the upper floors. (ラフォーレ; www.laforet.ne.jp; 1-11-6 Jingūmae, Shibuya-ku; ⏱11am-9pm; ⏚ JR Yamanote line to Harajuku, Omote-sandō exit)

Gallery Kawano   VINTAGE

23 MAP P106, C4

Gallery Kawano's selection of vintage kimonos are in good shape and priced reasonably (from ¥10,000). If you're serious about buying, the staff will help you pick out a matching obi and show you how to tie it. Crafty types can pick up kimono scrap fabric here, too. (ギャラリー川野; www.gallery-kawano.com; 4-4-9 Jingūmae, Shibuya-ku; ⏱11am-6pm; ⏚ Ginza line to Omote-sandō, exit A2)

KiddyLand   TOYS

24 MAP P106, B4

This multistorey toy emporium is packed to the rafters with character goods, including all your Studio Ghibli, Sanrio and Disney faves. It's not just for kids either; you'll spot plenty of adults on a nostalgia trip down the Hello Kitty aisle. (キデイランド; ☏03-3409-3431; www.kiddyland.co.jp; 6-1-9 Jingūmae, Shibuya-ku; ⏱11am-9pm Mon-Fri, 10.30am-9pm Sat & Sun; ⏚ JR Yamanote line to Harajuku, Omote-sandō exit)

Shinjuku

Shinjuku is a whole city within the city. Its breadth and scale are simply awesome – over three million people a day pass through the train station. To the west of the station is Nishi-Shinjuku, a planned district of soaring skyscrapers; to the east, the city's largest entertainment district, aglitter with coloured LED lights.

The Short List

o *Golden Gai (p116)* Dive into this beloved, bohemian night spot packed with tiny bars.

o *Tokyo Metropolitan Government Building (p119)* See for miles from the free 202m-high observatories atop Tokyo's city hall.

o *Shinjuku-gyoen (p119)* Laze on the lawn at this beloved urban oasis, a former imperial garden.

o *Godzilla Head (p119)* Pose with this enormous statue of Japanese film icon Godzilla, lording over Shinjuku.

o *Robot Restaurant (p122)* Experience OTT dazzling, eye-searing and overwhelming robot cabaret.

Getting There & Around

🚃 The JR Yamanote line and many others stop at Shinjuku.

Ⓢ Shinjuku-sanchōme is a useful subway stop, just east of Shinjuku Station (and near all the nightlife). It's serviced by the convenient east–west Marunouchi (red) line, which also stops at Nishi-Shinjuku (just west of Shinjuku Station) and Shinjuku-gyoenmae.

Neighbourhood Map on p118

Top Experience 📷

Bar-hop through Golden Gai

A Shinjuku institution for over half a century, Golden Gai (ゴールデン街) is a collection of some 200 tiny bars, seating maybe a dozen at most. Each is as unique and eccentric as the 'master' or 'mama' who runs it. In a sense, Golden Gai, which has a strong visual appeal, with its low-slung wooden buildings, is their work of art. It's more than just a place to drink.

◉ **MAP P118, E1**

http://goldengai.jp

1-1 Kabukichō, Shinjuku-ku

🚃 JR Yamanote line to Shinjuku, east exit

The History

Originally many bars functioned more like clubhouses for various creative people like artists and writers. Some bars still only welcome regulars to preserve that old atmosphere. Recently, as new, younger owners have taken over, the exclusive atmosphere of old is giving way to a lively scene of international bar-hoppers, instinctively drawn to Golden Gai's free spirit.

Recommended Bars

The best way to experience Golden Gai is to stroll the lanes and pick a place that suits your mood. A few suggestions to get you started:

Lonely (ロンリー; 1-1-8 Kabukichō, Shinjuku-ku; ⏱ 6.30pm-2am Tue-Sun) Akai-san established his cosy, eccentric and fun bar 50 years ago because he wanted his friends to always have a place to go. Some of those friends, like the creator of classic manga *Ashita no Joe* (you'll see posters on the wall) also happened to be famous.

La Jetée (ラジェッティ; ☎ 03-3208-9645; www.lajetee.org; 2nd fl, Hanazono 3-ban-gai, 1-1-8 Kabukichō, Shinjuku-ku; ⏱ 7pm-late Wed-Sat) Named for the Chris Marker film, this classic bar has been the go-to spot for film industry veterans (it appears in Wim Wenders' 1983 documentary *Tokyo-Ga*) for four decades.

Albatross G (アルバトロスG; www.alba-s.com; 5-ban gai, 1-1-7 Kabukichō, Shinjuku-ku; ⏱ 5pm-2am Sun-Thu, to 5am Fri & Sat) Dripping with chandeliers, this popular spot welcomes foreign visitors; it's also comparatively spacious, with three floors (try to get the table on the 3rd floor).

Open Book (Golden Gai 5-ban-gai, 1-1-6 Kabukichō, Shinjuku-ku; ⏱ 7pm-1.30am Mon-Sat) Run by the grandson of award-winning novelist Tanaka Komimasa (whose collection of well-loved books line the walls). The house special is an upgraded take on an old classic, the 'lemon sour' (*shōchū* distilled liquor, soda water and lemon juice; ¥700).

★ **Top Tips**

○ Bars that expressly welcome tourists have English signs posted on their doors. Note that most bars have a cover charge (usually ¥500 to ¥1500), which is often posted on the door.

○ The district is highly photogenic, but it's also private property. Do not take photos unless you have explicit permission.

○ The bars here get going late, say after 9pm.

🍴 **Take a Break**

It's not all bars here: indulge in the classic Tokyo late-night tradition of post-drinks ramen at **Nagi** (凪; ☎ 03-3205-1925; www.n-nagi.com; 2nd fl, Golden Gai G2, 1-1-10 Kabukichō, Shinjuku-ku; ramen from ¥890; ⏱ 24hr). The house speciality is *niboshi* ramen (egg noodles in a broth flavoured with dried sardines).

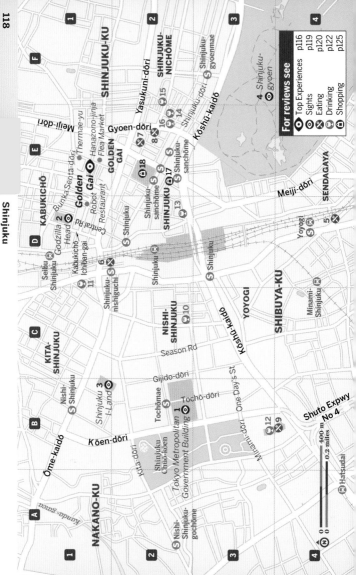

Shinjuku

Top Experiences

- SHINJUKU-KU
- KABUKICHŌ
- KITA-SHINJUKU
- NISHI-SHINJUKU
- SHINJUKU-NICHŌME
- SHINJUKU-SANCHŌME
- SHINJUKU
- YOYOGI
- SHIBUYA-KU
- NAKANO-KU
- SENDAGAYA

Kanda-gawa

Ōme-kaidō

Nishi-Shinjuku

Shinjuku 3 I-Land

Kōen-dōri

Shinjuku Chūō-kōen

Kita-dōri

Tokyo Metropolitan Government Building 1

Tochōmae

Tochō-dōri

Gijidō-dōri

Season Rd

Nishi-Shinjuku-gochōme

Kōshū-kaidō

One Day's St

Minami-dōri

Shuto Expwy No 4

Hatsudai

Hanazono-jinja Flea Market

Thermae-yu

Gyoen-dōri

GOLDEN GAI

Golden Gai

Robot Restaurant

Godzilla Head

Kabukichō Ichiban-gai

Central Rd

Bunka-Senta-dōri

Meiji-dōri

Yasukuni-dōri

Shinjuku-nichōme

Shinjuku-gyoenmae

Shinjuku-dōri

Kōshū-kaidō

Shinjuku-sanchōme

Meiji-dōri

Yoyogi

Minami-Shinjuku

Seibu Shinjuku

Shinjuku-nishiguchi

Shinjuku

Shinjuku

Shinjuku

4 Shinjuku-gyoen

For reviews see

- ⊙ Top Experiences   p116
- ⊙ Sights   p119
- ⊗ Eating   p120
- ⊙ Drinking   p122
- ⊙ Shopping   p125

0   400 m
0   0.2 miles

N

Sights

Tokyo Metropolitan Government Building

OBSERVATORY

1 ◎ MAP P118, B2

Tokyo's city hall – a landmark building designed by Tange Kenzō – has observatories (202m) atop both the south and north towers of Building 1 (the views are virtually the same). On a clear day (morning is best), you may catch a glimpse of Mt Fuji to the west, beyond the urban sprawl; after dark, it's illuminated buildings all the way to the horizon. Direct-access elevators are on the ground floor; last entry is at 10.30pm. (東京都庁; Tokyo Tochō; www.metro.tokyo.jp/english/offices; 2-8-1 Nishi-Shinjuku, Shinjuku-ku; admission free; ⊙observatories 9.30am-11pm; Ⓢ Ōedo line to Tochōmae, exit A4)

Godzilla Head

STATUE

2 ◎ MAP P118, D1

Godzilla, a portmanteau of the Japanese words for gorilla (gorira) and whale (kujira), is king of the kaijū (strange beasts) that ruled Japanese popular cinema for decades. This giant statue of him looking to take a bite out of a skyscraper has become a Shinjuku landmark. Every so often he roars to life, with glowing eyes and smoky breath. (ゴジラヘッド; Shinjuku Toho Bldg, 1-19-1 Kabukichō, Shinjuku-ku; ⊙Godzilla Terrace 6.30am-9pm; ℝJR Yamanote line to Shinjuku, east exit)

Shinjuku I-Land

PUBLIC ART

3 ◎ MAP P118, B1

This otherwise ordinary office complex is home to more than a dozen public artworks, including one of Robert Indiana's LOVE sculptures (on the southeast corner) and two Tokyo Brushstroke sculptures by Roy Lichtenstein (at the back, towards Ōme-kaidō). The open-air courtyard, with stonework by Giulio Paolini and several reasonably priced restaurants, makes an attractive lunch or coffee stop. (新宿 アイランド; 6-5-1 Nishi-Shinjuku, Shinjuku-ku; Ⓢ Marunouchi line to Nishi-Shinjuku)

Shinjuku-gyoen

PARK

4 ◎ MAP P118, F3

Shinjuku-gyoen was designed as an imperial retreat (completed 1906); since opening to the public in 1951, it's become a favourite destination for Tokyoites in need of a quick escape from the hurly-burly of city life. The spacious manicured lawns are perfect for picnicking. Don't miss the greenhouse; the Taiwanese-style pavilion (Goryō-tei) that overlooks the garden's central pond; and the cherry blossoms in spring. (新宿御苑; ☎03-3350-0151; www.env.go.jp/garden/shinjukugyoen; 11 Naito-chō, Shinjuku-ku; adult/child ¥200/50; ⊙9am-4.30pm Tue-Sun; Ⓢ Marunouchi line to Shinjuku-gyoen-mae, exit 1)

Omoide-yokochō

Eating

Gochisō Tonjiru

JAPANESE ¥

5  MAP P118, D4

Tonjiru, a home-cooking classic, is a hearty miso soup packed with root veggies (such as burdock root, *daikon*, potato and carrot) and chunks of pork. At this neighbourhood hang-out, styled more like a bar than a restaurant, the pork comes in the form of melting-off-the-bone barbecued spare ribs. Choose between a Kyoto-style light miso or a Tokyo-style dark miso. (ごちそうとん汁; ☎03-6883-9181; 1-33-2 Yoyogi, Shibuya-ku; meals from ¥840; ⊙11.30am-midnight; 🚆JR Yamanote line to Yoyogi, west exit)

Omoide-yokochō

YAKITORI ¥

6  MAP P118, D1

Literally 'Memory Lane' (and less politely known as Shonben-yokochō, or 'Piss Alley'), Omoide-yokochō started as a post-war black market and somehow managed to stick around. Today, it's one of Tokyo's most recognisable sights. There are dozens of small restaurants, mostly serving *yakitori* (chicken, and other meats or vegetables, grilled on skewers), packed into the alley here; several have English menus. (思い出横丁; Nishi-Shinjuku 1-chōme, Shinjuku-ku; skewers from ¥150; ⊙varies by shop; 🚆JR Yamanote line to Shinjuku, west exit)

Kanae
IZAKAYA ¥¥

7 🗺 MAP P118, E2

Kanae is a perfect example of one of Shinjuku-sanchōme's excellent and all but undiscoverable *izakaya* (Japanese pub-eatery): delicious sashimi, seasonal dishes and simple staples (the potato salad is famous) in the basement of an unremarkable building (there's a white sign with a sake barrel out front). Seating is at the counter or at a handful of tables; reservations recommended. (鼎; ☎050-3467-1376; basement fl, 3-12-12 Shinjuku, Shinjuku-ku; cover charge ¥540; dishes ¥660-1980; ⏰5pm-midnight Mon-Sat, 4.30-11pm Sun; 🚉JR Yamanote line to Shinjuku, east exit)

Donjaca
IZAKAYA ¥¥

8 🗺 MAP P118, E2

Donjaca, in business since 1979, has many telltale signs of a classic Shōwa-era (1926–89) *izakaya* red vinyl stools, lantern lighting and hand-written menus covering the wall. The food is equal parts classic (grilled fish and fried chicken) and inventive: a house speciality is *natto gyoza* (dumplings stuffed with fermented soybeans). Excellent sake, too. (呑者家; ☎03-3341-2497; 3-9-10 Shinjuku, Shinjuku-ku; cover charge ¥300, dishes ¥350-900; ⏰5pm-7am; 🚇Marunouchi line to Shinjuku-sanchōme, exit C6)

Shinjuku Cleanup

The best (and most literal) example to date that red-light district Kabukichō is cleaning up its act: **Thermae-yu** (テルマー湯; Map p118, E1; ☎03-5285-1726; www.thermae-yu.jp; 1-1-2 Kabukichō, Shinjuku-ku; weekdays/weekends & holidays ¥2365/2690; ⏰11am-9am; 🚉JR Yamanote line to Shinjuku, east exit), a sparkling-clean onsen complex. The tubs, which include several indoor and outdoor ones (gender-segregated), are filled with honest-to-goodness natural hot-spring water. There are several saunas, including a hot-stone sauna (*ganbanyoku*, ¥810 extra). Towels included. No tattoos allowed.

Kozue
JAPANESE ¥¥¥

9 🗺 MAP P118, B4

It's hard to beat Kozue's combination of exquisite seasonal Japanese cuisine, artisan crockery and distractingly good views over Shinjuku. As the (kimono-clad) staff speak English and the restaurant caters well to dietary restrictions and personal preferences, this is a good splurge spot for diners who don't want to give up complete control. Reservations essential for dinner and recommended for lunch; 15% service charge. (梢; ☎03-5323-3460;

Robot Restaurant 🍴

This Kabukichō **spectacle** (ロボットレストラン; Map p118, D1; 📞03-3200-5500; www.shinjuku-robot.com; 1-7-1 Kabukichō, Shinjuku-ku; tickets ¥8000; ⏰shows at 5.55pm, 7.50pm & 9.45pm, additional show at 4pm Fri-Sun; 🚊JR Yamanote line to Shinjuku, east exit) has hit it big with its vision of 'wacky Japan': bikini-clad women ride around on giant robots against a backdrop of animated screens and enough LED lights to illuminate all of Shinjuku. You can book ahead online (at full price) or save up to ¥2000 per person by purchasing at the venue with a discount flyer (available at TICs and hotels).

www.hyatt.com; 40th fl, Park Hyatt Tokyo, 3-7-1-2 Nishi-Shinjuku, Shinjuku-ku; lunch set menu ¥2480-10,800, dinner set menu ¥14,040-24,850; ⏰11.30am-2.30pm & 5.30-9.30pm; 🚇Ōedo line to Tochōmae, exit A4)

Drinking

BenFiddich
COCKTAIL BAR

10 🚇 MAP P118, C2

BenFiddich is dark and tiny, with vials of infusions on the shelves and herbs hung to dry from the ceiling. The English-speaking barman, Kayama Hiroyasu, in a white suit, moves like a magician. There's no menu, so just tell him what you like and he'll concoct something delicious for you (we like the gimlet with herbs). Expect to pay around ¥2000 per drink. (ベンフィディック; 📞03-6279-4223; 9th fl, 1-13-7 Nishi-Shinjuku, Shinjuku-ku; ⏰6pm-3am Mon-Sat; 🚊JR Yamanote line to Shinjuku, west exit)

Zoetrope
BAR

11 🚇 MAP P118, D1

A must-visit for whisky fans, Zoetrope has some 300 varieties of Japanese whisky behind its small counter – including hard-to-find bottles from small-batch distilleries. It's a one-man show and the owner speaks English well. Cover charge ¥600; whisky by the glass from ¥400 to ¥19,000, though most are reasonably priced (around ¥800 to ¥1200), and there are some good-value tasting flights, too. (ゾートロープ; 📞03-3363-0162; 3rd fl, 7-10-14 Nishi-Shinjuku, Shinjuku-ku; ⏰5pm-midnight Mon-Sat; 🚊JR Yamanote line to Shinjuku, west exit)

Eagle
GAY

There's much to love about the Shinjuku-nichōme bar Eagle (see 14 🚇 Map p118, E2): the friendly staff, the happy-hour prices (¥500 drinks from 5pm to 8pm; otherwise they're ¥700), but especially the instantly iconic mural from proudly out manga artist Inuyoshi. Pick up a free copy of the artist's bilingual manga *Nippondanji* here. (www.eagletokyo.com; 2-12-3 Shinjuku, Shinjuku-ku; ⏰6pm-1am Sun-Thu, to 4am Fri & Sat; 🚊JR Yamanote line to Shinjuku, east exit)

View from the Tokyo Metropolitan Government Building (p119)

Peak Bar

BAR

12 MAP P118, B3

The Peak Bar offers soaring views over the city and a generous deal: its three-hour (5pm to 8pm) all-you-can-drink plus unlimited canapés 'Twilight Time' special costs just ¥6000 (tax and service charge included). Okay, that's still a fair amount, but we're talking the Park Hyatt here! Otherwise cocktails start from ¥1950 (plus a 15% service charge). DJs spin Wednesday through Saturday from 6pm. Dress code enforced. (ピークバー; 03-5323-3461; http://restaurants.tokyo.park.hyatt.co.jp/en/pbr.html; 41st fl, Park Hyatt, 3-7-1-2 Nishi-Shinjuku, Shinjuku-ku; 5-11.30pm; Ōedo line to Tochōmae, exit A4)

Samurai

BAR

13 MAP P118, D2

Never mind the impressive record collection, this eccentric jazz *kissa* (cafe where jazz records are played) is worth a visit just for the owner's overwhelming collection of 2500 *maneki-neko* (beckoning cats). It's on the alleyway alongside the highway, with a small sign on the front of the building. There's a ¥300 cover charge (¥500 after 9pm); drinks from ¥650. (サムライ; http://jazz-samurai.seesaa.net; 5th fl, 3-35-5 Shinjuku, Shinjuku-ku; 6pm-1am; JR Yamanote line to Shinjuku, southeast exit)

Bar Goldfinger GAY & LESBIAN

14 MAP P118, E2

Goldfinger is a long-running ladies' spot in Shinjuku-nichōme (but open to all, save for Saturdays). The bar has a lowbrow-chic decor designed to look like a '70s motel, a friendly vibe and fun events, like Friday-night karaoke. Drinks from ¥700; no cover unless there's an event. (☎03-6383-4649; www. goldfingerparty.com; 2-12-11 Shinjuku, Shinjuku-ku; ☺6pm-2am Sun-Thu, to 5am Fri & Sat; ⓢMarunouchi line to Shinjuku-sanchōme, exit C8)

Aiiro Cafe GAY & LESBIAN

15 MAP P118, F2

Aiiro is the best place to start any night out in Shinjuku-nichōme, thanks to the all-you-can-drink beer for ¥1000 happy-hour special from 6pm to 9pm daily. The bar itself is teeny-tiny; the action happens on the street corner outside, which swells to block-party proportions when the weather is nice. There's a red *torii* (gate) out front; you can't miss it. (アイイロカフェ; ☎03-6273-0740; www.aliving. net; 2-18-1 Shinjuku, Shinjuku-ku; ☺6pm-2am Mon-Thu, to 5am Fri & Sat, to midnight Sun; ⓢMarunouchi line to Shinjuku-sanchōme, exit C8)

Arty Farty GAY & LESBIAN

16 MAP P118, E2

A fixture on Tokyo's gay scene for many a moon, Arty Farty welcomes all in the community to come shake a tail feather on its (admittedly small) dance floor. It gets going later in the evening.

Isetan

Weekend events sometimes have a cover charge (¥1000 to ¥2000), which includes entrance to sister club, **The Annex**, around the corner. Drinks from ¥700. (アーティファーティ; ☎03-5362-9720; www.arty-farty.net; 2nd fl, 2-11-7 Shinjuku, Shinjuku-ku; ⏰8pm-4am Sun-Thu, to 5am Fri & Sat; Ⓢ Marunouchi line to Shinjuku-sanchōme, exit C8)

Shopping

Beams Japan   FASHION & ACCESSORIES

17 🔒 MAP P118, E2

Beams, a national chain of trend-setting boutiques, is a Japanese cultural institution and this multi-storey Shinjuku branch has a particular audience in mind: you, the traveller. It's full of the latest Japanese streetwear labels, traditional fashions with cool modern twists, artisan crafts, pop art and more – all contenders for that perfect only-in-Tokyo souvenir. Warning: set your budget before you enter. (ビームス・ジャパン; www.beams.co.jp; 3-32-6 Shinjuku, Shinjuku-ku; ⏰11am-8pm; 🚇JR Yamanote line to Shinjuku, east exit)

Isetan   DEPARTMENT STORE

18 🔒 MAP P118, E2

Isetan is our favourite Tokyo department store for several

Hanazono-jinja Flea Market

At this long-running **market** (青空骨董市, Aozora Kottō-ichi; Map p118, E1; http://kottou-ichi.jp; Hanazono-jinja, 5-17 Shinjuku, Shinjuku-ku; ⏰dawn-dusk Sun; Ⓢ Marunouchi line to Shinjuku-sanchōme, exits B10 & E2) on the grounds of Hanazono-jinja, vendors deal in antiques, old prints, used kimonos and more. You'd have to have a professional eye to score a real deal, but pretty lacquer trays and ceramic sake cups can be found for around ¥1000. Best to go early. Cancelled in the event of rain or a competing shrine festival.

reasons: the up-and-coming Japanese fashion designers (check the 2nd-floor Tokyo Closet and 3rd-floor Re-Style boutiques in the main building, and the 2nd floor of the men's building); the homewares from contemporary artisans (5th floor); and the quite literally mouthwatering *depachika* (basement food hall). (伊勢丹; ☎03-3352-1111; www.isetan.co.jp; 3-14-1 Shinjuku, Shinjuku-ku; ⏰10.30am-8pm; Ⓢ Marunouchi line to Shinjuku-sanchōme, exits B3, B4 & B5)

Worth a Trip 🔭
Enter the world of Ghibli Museum, Mitaka

Since 1986, master animator Miyazaki Hayao and his Studio Ghibli (pronounced ji-bu-ri) have been responsible for some of the best-loved films in Japan – and the world. Miyazaki designed the museum himself, and it's redolent of the dreamy atmosphere that makes his animations so enchanting. Tickets must be purchased in advance, and you must choose the exact time and date you plan to visit.

ジブリ美術館
www.ghibli-museum.jp

1-1-83 Shimo-Renjaku, Mitaka-shi

adult ¥1000, child ¥100-700

🕙10am-6pm Wed-Mon

🚉JR Chūō-Sōbu line to Mitaka, south exit

Get to Know Ghibli

If you've seen a Ghibli movie, odds are it was 2001's *Spirited Away*, which won the Academy Award for Best Animated Feature (and remains the only Japanese animated film and only hand-drawn film ever to win). Here's a chance to further explore Ghibli's world: inside the museum is an imagined workshop filled with the kinds of books and artworks that inspired Miyazaki. There's also a small theatre where original animated shorts – which can only be seen here! – are screened (you'll get a ticket for this when you enter).

Meet Friends Old & New

The Ghibli Museum, Mitaka rewards curiosity and play: peer through a small window, for example, and you'll see little soot sprites (as seen in *Spirited Away*). A spiral staircase leads to a purposefully overgrown rooftop terrace with a 5m tall statue of the Robot Soldier from *Laputa* (Castle in the Sky; 1986). A highlight for children (sorry, grown-ups!) is a giant, plush replica of the cat bus from the classic *My Neighbor Totoro* (1988) that kids can climb on.

Nearby: Inokashira-kōen

The Ghibli Museum, Mitaka is actually in the corner of one of Tokyo's best parks, **Inokashira-kōen** (井の頭公園; www.kensetsu. metro.tokyo.jp/seibuk/inokashira/index.html; 1-18-31 Gotenyama, Musashino-shi; ⬛JR Chūō-Sōbu line to Kichijōji, Kōen exit). Instead of heading back to Mitaka Station, walk through the park to Kichijōji Station (also on the JR Chūō line). The walk takes about 30 minutes; it's signposted in English. Along the way you'll pass a big pond with an island that's home to an ancient shrine to the sea goddess Benzaiten.

★ Top Tips

○ Tickets sell out fast, especially during the school holidays.

○ Buy tickets up to four months in advance from a travel agent; it's the best open, as you can reserve earlier.

○ Otherwise get tickets a month in advance from convenience store Lawson's online ticket portal; details are on the website.

✖ Take a Break

The museum has its own restaurant, but it's routinely packed. Instead, walk through Inokashira-kōen to **Blue Sky Coffee** (ブルースカイコーヒー; 4-12 Inokashira, Mitaka-shi; coffee from ¥250; ⏱10am-6pm Thu-Tue; 📷; ⬛Keiō Inokashira line to Inokashira-kōen).

★ Getting There

🚌 Take the JR Chūō line from Shinjuku to Mitaka. From the south exit no 9 bus stop, get a shuttle bus (round trip/one way ¥320/210; every 20 minutes).

Explore ◈

Kagurazaka, Kōrakuen & Around

The old geisha district of Kagurazaka is one of Tokyo's most charming areas for shopping and dining. Nearby Kōrakuen is home to the serene traditional garden Koishikawa Kōrakuen and the baseball stadium Tokyo Dome, hub of a fun amusement park. Further east are the electronic, pop-culture and contemporary-craft emporiums of Akihabara.

The Short List

○ **Koishikawa Kōrakuen (p135)** *Visit a classic traditional garden with seasonal flowerings.*

○ **Kanda Myōjin (p135)** *Make your way to this venerable Shintō shrine, which hosts one of Tokyo's top festivals.*

○ **Kagurazaka (p130)** *Navigate the stone-flagged streets of this old geisha quarter.*

○ **TeNQ (p135)** *Enjoy this fun, educational museum focusing on space science.*

○ **Toyokuni Atelier Gallery (p135)** *Try your hand at sumie, the art of ink painting.*

Getting There & Around

🚃 JR trains stop at Akihabara, Iidabashi (for Kagurazaka) and Suidōbashi (for Kōrakuen).

Ⓢ The Hibiya line stops near Akihabara, while the Ginza line stops at Suehirochō. Other useful stations include Iidabashi, Kōrakuen and Kagurazaka.

Neighbourhood Map on p134

Koishikawa Kōrakuen (p135) TAKASHI IMAGES / SHUTTERSTOCK ©

Walking Tour

Kagurazaka

At the start of the 20th century, Kagurazaka was a fashionable hanamachi – a pleasure quarter where geisha entertained. Though there are far fewer geisha today (they're seldom seen by tourists), the neighbourhood retains its glamour and charm. It's a popular destination for Tokyoites, who enjoy wandering the cobblestone lanes or whiling away time in one of the area's many cafes.

Walk Facts

Start Geisha Shinmichi; Iidabashi Station, west exit

End Akagi-jinja; S Kagurazaka Station, exit 1

Length 1km; one hour

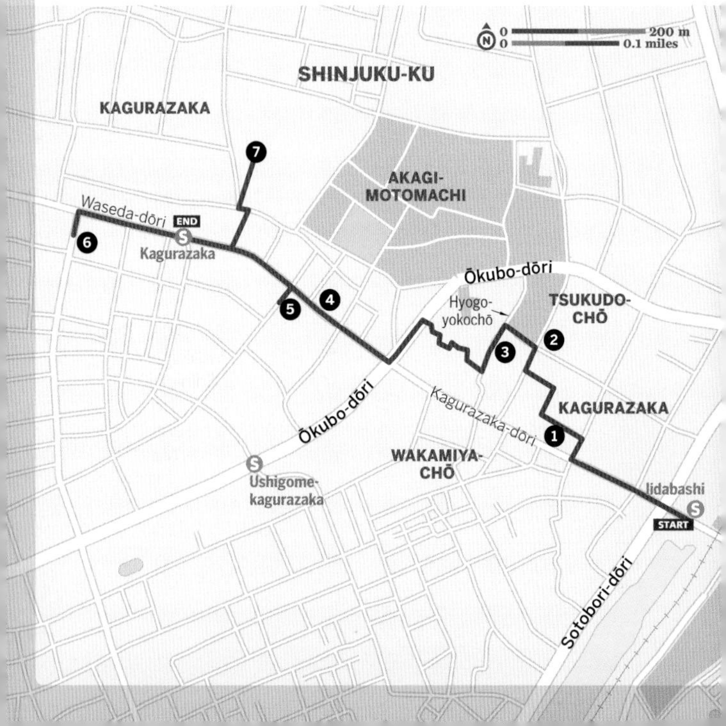

❶ Geisha Shinmichi

Walk up Kagurazaka-dōri, turn right at Royal Host restaurant and then take the first left onto Geisha Shinmichi. This narrow lane was once where geisha lived and worked. Though it's now home to residences and restaurants, the paving stones remain.

❷ Kukuli

At the end of attractive side-street Honta-yokochō is **Kukuli** (くくり; ☏03-6280-8462; www.kukuli. co.jp; 1-10 Tsukudo-chō, Shinjuku-ku; ⏰11am-7pm), one of several shops specialising in traditional craft-work. It has hand-dyed textiles (such as scarves and tea towels) with a modern touch.

❸ Hyogo-yokochō

Winding cobblestone alley Hyogo-yokochō is the neighbourhood's oldest and most atmospheric lane, often used in TV and movie shoots. You'll see *ryōtei* here: exclusive, traditional Japanese restaurants (for which Kagurazaka is famous).

❹ Baikatei

Award-winning, 80-year-old confectioner **Baikatei** (梅花亭; ☏03-5228-0727; www.baikatei. co.jp; 6-15 Kagurazaka, Shinjuku-ku; ⏰10am-8pm, to 7.30pm Sun) turns out gorgeous *wagashi* (Japanese-style sweets). Watch the chefs at work, whipping humble beans and rice into pastel flowers, from the window in the back.

❺ Sada

The ever-changing selection at **Sada** (貞; ☏03-3513-0851; www. sadakagura.com; 6-58 Kagurazaka, Shinjuku-ku; ⏰noon-7pm) includes clothes and pretty accessories handmade in Japan. Some items are contemporary; others have a traditional Japanese feel, made with kimono material.

❻ La Kagu

Take a rest on the terrace steps outside **La Kagu** (ラカグ; ☏03-5227-6977; www.lakagu.com; 67 Yarai-chō, Shinjuku-ku; ⏰11am-8.30pm), an old book warehouse, revamped by architect Kengo Kuma into a lifestyle boutique stocking a keenly edited range of fashion and homewares. There's also a cafe here.

❼ Akagi-jinja

Akagi-jinja (赤城神社; ☏03-3260-5071; ⏰9am-5pm; www.akagi-jinja.jp; 1-10 Akagi-Motomachi, Shinjuku-ku), Kagurazaka's signature shrine, only bears a passing resemblance to the traditional ones around the city. In 2010 the shrine, which can trace its history back centuries, was remodelled by Kengo Kuma, one of Japan's most prominent architects. The result is a sleek glass box.

Walking Tour 🥾

An Afternoon in Akihabara

Akihabara (Akiba to friends) is Tokyo's otaku (geek) subculture centre. But you don't have to obsess about manga (Japanese comics) or anime (Japanese animation) to enjoy this quirky neighbourhood. It's equal parts sensory overload and cultural mind-bender. In fact, as the otaku subculture gains more influence on the culture at large, Akiba is drawing more visitors who don't fit the stereotype.

Getting There

🚃 The JR Yamanote and Sōbu lines stop at Akihabara; Electric Town exit is the most convenient.

Ⓢ The Hibiya line stops at Akihabara; take exit 3.

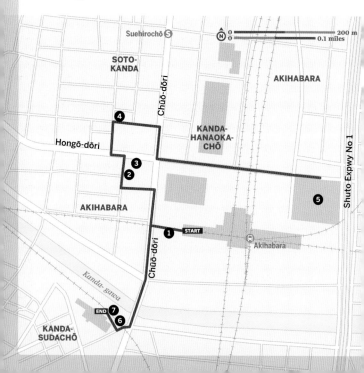

❶ Electric Town

Before Akihabara became *otaku*-land, it was Electric Town – the place for discounted electronics and where early computer geeks tracked down obscure parts for home-built machines. **Akihabara Radio Center** (秋葉原ラジオセンター; www.radiocenter.jp; 1-14-2 Soto-Kanda, Chiyoda-ku; ⏰generally 10am-6pm), a warren of stalls under the train tracks, keeps the tradition alive.

❷ Vintage Arcade Games

In Akihabara, a love of the new is tempered with a deep affection for the old. **Super Potato Retro-kan** (スーパーポテトレトロ館; 📞03-5289 9933; www.superpotato.com; 1-11-2 Soto-kanda, Chiyoda-ku; ⏰11am-8pm Mon-Fri, from 10am Sat & Sun) is a retro video arcade with some old-school consoles.

❸ Maid Cafe

Maid cafes – where waitresses dress as French maids and treat customers with giggling deference as *go-shujinsama* (master) or *o-jōsama* (miss) – are an Akiba institution. Pop into **@Home** (@ほぉ～むカフェ; 📞03-3255-2808; www.cafe-athome.com; 4th-7th fl, 1-11-4 Soto-Kanda, Chiyoda-ku; ⏰11am-10pm Mon-Fri, from 10am Sat & Sun; 📷) for a game of *moe moe jankan* (rock, paper, scissors) maid-style.

❹ Mandarake Complex

To get an idea of what *otaku* obsess over, a trip to Mandarake Complex (p138) will do the trick. It's eight storeys of comic books and DVDs, action figures and cel art.

❺ Yodobashi-Akiba

The modern avatar of Akihabara Radio Center is **Yodobashi-Akiba** (ヨドバシカメラAkibi; 📞03-5209 1010; www.yodobashi-akiba.com; 1-1 Kanda Hanaoka-chō, Chiyoda-ku; ⏰9.30am-10pm), a monster electronics store beloved by camera junkies.

❻ MAAch ecute

MAAch ecute (📞03-3257-8910; www.ecute.jp/maach; 1-25-4 Kanda-Sudachō, Chiyoda-ku; ⏰11am-9pm Mon-Sat, to 8pm Sun) is a shopping and dining complex, crafted from the old station and railway arches of Mansei-bashi, selling homewares, fashion and food.

❼ Hitachino Brewing Lab

Sake brewery Kiuchi has been brewing its excellent range of Hitachino Nest craft beers since 1996. Work your way from its white beer to the sweet stout while gazing across the Kanda-gawa seating at this dedicated **bar** (📞03-3254 3434; http://hitachino.cc; 1-25-4 Kanda-Sudachō, Chiyoda-ku; ⏰11am-11pm Mon-Sat, to 9pm Sun).

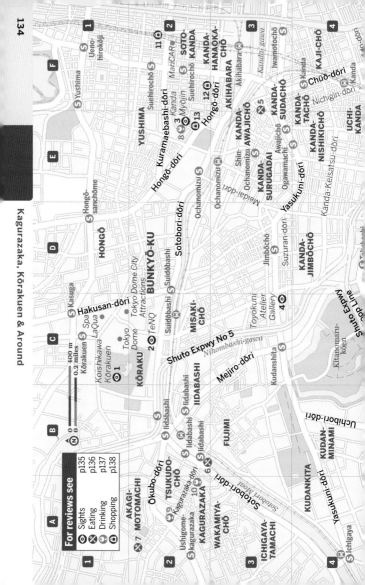

Kagurazaka, Kōrakuen & Around

For reviews see

◎	Sights	p135
⊗	Eating	p136
⊗	Drinking	p137
⊕	Shopping	p138

0 400 m
0 0.2 miles

A

AKAGI-
MOTOMACHI

Ōkubo-dōri

Ushigome-S kagurazaka

TSUKUDO-
CHŌ

Kagurazaka-dōri

KAGURAZAKA

WAKAMIYA-
CHŌ

ICHIGAYA-
TAMACHI

B

Iidabashi S

Iidabashi S

Iidabashi

FUJIMI

Sotobori-dōri

Sotobori-gawa

KUDANKITA

Yasukuni-dōri

Ichigaya

KUDAN-
MINAMI

Uchibori-dōri

C

Kasuga S

Hakusan-dōri

Koishikawa
Kōrakuen

Tokyo
Dome

Spa
LaQua S

Tokyo Dome City
Attractions

TeNQ

KŌRAKU-
EN

Suidōbashi

Shuto Expwy No 5

Nihombashi-gawa

Mejiro-dōri

Kudanshita S

Shuto Expwy

Kitanomaru-
kōen

D

Hongō-
sanchōme S

HONGŌ

BUNKYŌ-KU

Suidōbashi S

MISAKI-
CHŌ

Jimbōchō S

KANDA-
JIMBŌCHŌ

Suzuran-dōri

E

Yushima S

YUSHIMA

Suehirochō S

Kuramaebashi-dōri

Hongō-dōri

Sotobori-dōri

Ochanomizu S

Ochanomizu

Meidai-dōri

Shin-
Ochanomizu S

KANDA-
SURUGADAI

Ogawamachi S

Awajichō

KANDA-
NISHIKICHŌ

Yasukuni-dōri

Kanda-Keisatsu-dōri

F

Ueno-
hirokōji S

Suehirochō 2

MariCARⓣ

SOTO-
KANDA

KANDA-
HANAOKA-
CHŌ

AKIHABARA

Akihabara S

Kanda
Myōjin

Iwamotochō S

Kanda-gawa

Hongō-dōri

KANDA-
AWAJICHŌ

KANDA
SUDACHŌ

KANDA-
TACHŌ

Nichigin-dōri

Chūō-dōri

KAJI-CHŌ

Kanda S

UCHI-
KANDA

11

12

3

8

13

9

10

7

2

1

6

4

5

Sights

Koishikawa Kōrakuen   GARDENS

1 ⊙ MAP P134, C1

Established in the mid-17th century as the property of the Tokugawa clan, this formal strolling garden incorporates elements of Chinese and Japanese landscaping. It's among Tokyo's most attractive gardens, although nowadays the *shakkei* (borrowed scenery) also includes the contemporary skyline of Tokyo Dome (p138). (小石川後楽園; ☏03-3811-3015; www.tokyo-park.or.jp/teien; 1-6-6 Kōraku, Bunkyō-ku; adult/child ¥300/free; ⊙9am-5pm; ⍟Ōedo line to Iidabashi, exit C3)

TeNQ   MUSEUM

2 ⊙ MAP P134, C2

This nifty, interactive museum is devoted to outer-space exploration and science. Timed entry tickets start you off with one of three impressive high-resolution videos projected across an 11m-diameter screen that you stand around. Good English captions throughout make it a fine educational experience. Set aside a couple of hours to do the museum justice. (テンキュー; ☏03-3814-0109; www.tokyo-dome.co.jp; 6F Tokyo Dome City, Yellow Bldg, 1-3-61 Kōraku, Bunkyō-ku; adult/child ¥1800/1200; ⊙11am-9pm Mon-Fri, from 10am Sat & Sun; 🚼; ⍟JR Sōbu line to Suidōbashi, west exit)

Kanda Myōjin   SHINTO SHRINE

3 ⊙ MAP P134, E2

Tracing its history back to AD 730, this splendid Shintō shrine boasts vermilion-lacquered halls surrounding a stately courtyard. Its present location dates from 1616 and the *kami* (gods) enshrined here are said to bring luck in business and in finding a spouse. There are also plenty of anime characters, since this is Akiba's local shrine. (神田明神, Kanda Shrine; ☏03-3254-0753; www.kandamyoujin.or.jp; 2-16-2 Soto-kanda, Chiyoda-ku; admission free; ⍟JR Chūō or Sōbu lines to Ochano-mizu, Hijiri-bashi exit)

Toyokuni Atelier Gallery   ARTS & CRAFTS

4 ⊙ MAP P134, C3

Get a taster of *sumie,* the delicate art of ink painting on *washi* (Japanese handmade paper), at this gallery displaying the artworks of master ink painter Honda Toyokuni. The one-hour class is taught by his English-speaking, affable son Yuta, and highly recommended for budding artists of all ages. Reservations are essential. (豊國アトリエ; ☏090-4069-8410; www.nekomachi.com; 3-1-13 Kanda-Jimbōchō, Chiyoda-ku; 1hr class ¥2000; ⊙gallery noon-5pm Tue-Thu, Sat & Sun, classes 1pm, 3pm or 5pm; �startS Shinjuku line to Jimbōchō, exit A1)

Guardian statues at Kanda Myōjin (p135)

Eating

Kanda Yabu Soba

SOBA ¥

5 MAP P134, F3

Totally rebuilt following a fire in 2013, this is one of Tokyo's most venerable buckwheat noodle shops, in business since 1880. Come here for classic handmade noodles and accompaniments such as shrimp tempura (ten-seiro soba) or slices of duck (kamo-nanban soba). (神田やぶそば; 03-3251-0287; www.yabusoba. net; 2-10 Kanda-Awajichō, Chiyoda-ku; noodles ¥670-1910; 11.30am-8.30pm Thu-Tue; S Marunouchi line to Awajichō, exit A3)

Canal Cafe

ITALIAN ¥¥

6 MAP P134, B2

Along a languid stretch of what was once the outer moat of Edo Castle, this is one of Tokyo's best al fresco dining spots. The restaurant serves tasty wood-fired pizzas, seafood pastas and grilled meats, while over on the self-service 'deck side' you can settle in with a sandwich, a muffin or just a cup of coffee. (カナルカフェ; 03-3260-8068; www.canalcafe. jp; 1-9 Kagurazaka, Shinjuku-ku; lunch from ¥800, dinner mains ¥1600-2800; 11.30am-11pm Tue-Sat, to 9.30pm Sun; ; R JR Sōbu line to Iidabashi, west exit)

MariCAR
Karting Tours

Experience Tokyo as if in a real-life video game on fun go-karting tours around the city where you can dress up in brightly coloured onesies. For these tours organised by **MariCAR** (マリカー; Map p134, F2; ☏080-8899-8899; https://maricar.com; 4-12-9 Soto-Kanda, Chiyoda-ku; 1/2/3hr tours ¥5000/7500/10,000; ◷10am-8pm; ⒮Ginza line to Suehirochō, exit 1), you must, however, have a valid International Driving Permit (or a Japanese driver's licence). The two-hour course will get you out to Tokyo Skytree and down to Ginza. Apart from Akihabara, MariCAR also has shops in Shibuya, Asakusa, Shinagawa and Shin-Kiba – each one offering different driving courses.

Kado   JAPANESE ¥¥

7 🍴 MAP P134, A2

Set in an old wooden house with a white lantern out the front, Kado specialises in *katei-ryōri* (home-cooking). Dinner is a set course of seasonal dishes (such as grilled quail or fresh tofu). Bookings are required for the full selection of courses, but you can try turning up on the night and if there's space, you'll be able to eat. (カド; ☏03-3268-2410; http://kagurazaka-kado.com; 1-32 Akagi-Motomachi, Shinjuku-ku; set menus ¥3000-5000; ◷restaurant 5-11pm Tue-Fri, bar from 4pm Tue-Fri, from 2pm Sat & Sun; 🚇Tōzai line to Kagurazaka, exit 1)

Drinking

Imasa   CAFE

8 ☕ MAP P134, E2

It's not every day you get to sip your coffee or tea in a cultural property. Imasa is the real deal, an old timber merchant's shophouse dating from 1927 but with Edo-era design and detail, and a few pieces of contemporary furniture. Very few houses like this exist in Tokyo or are open to the public. (井政; ☏03-3255-3565; www.kanda-imasa.co.jp; 2-16 Soto-Kanda, Chiyoda-ku; drinks ¥600; ◷11am-4pm Mon-Fri; 🚉JR Chūō or Sōbu lines to Ochano-mizu, Hijiri-bashi exit)

Mugimaru 2   CAFE

9 ☕ MAP P134, A2

This old house, completely covered in ivy, is a charmer with a welcoming owner and two of Tokyo's most famous shop cats. Seating is on floor cushions; warm, squishy *manjū* (steamed buns) are the house speciality. It's in a tangle of alleys just off Ōkubo-dōri; you'll know it when you see it. (ムギマル 2; ☏03-5228-6393; www.mugimaru2.com; 5-20 Kagurazaka, Shinjuku-ku; coffee ¥550; ◷noon-9pm Thu-Tue; ⒮Tōzai line to Kagurazaka, exit 1)

Craft Beer Server Land

CRAFT BEER

10 🚇 MAP P134, A2

With some 14 Japanese craft beers on tap, going for a reasonable ¥500/840 a glass/pint, plus good food (the deep-fried eel in batter and chips is excellent), this brightly lit basement bar with wooden furniture and a slight Scandi feel is a winner. (📞03-6228-1891; Okawa Bldg B1F, 2-9 Kagurazaka, Shinjuku-ku; service charge ¥380; ⏰5pm-midnight Mon-Fri, from noon Sat & Sun; 📶; 🚉JR Sōbu line to Iidabashi, west exit)

Shopping

2k540 Aki-Oka Artisan

ARTS & CRAFTS

11 🔒 MAP P134, F2

This ace arcade under the JR tracks (its name refers to the distance from Tokyo Station) offers an eclectic range of stores selling Japanese-made goods – everything from pottery and leatherwork to cute aliens, a nod to Akihabara from a mall that is more akin to Kyoto than Electric Town. The best spot for colourful crafts is **Nippon Hyakkaten** (日本百貨店; http://nippon-dept.jp). (アキオカアルチザン; 📞03-6806 0254; www.jrtk.jp/2k540; 5-9-23 Ueno, Taitō-ku; ⏰11am-7pm Thu-Tue; 🚉Ginza line to Suehirochō, exit 2)

Mandarake Complex

MANGA & ANIME

12 🔒 MAP P134, F2

When *otaku* (geeks) dream of heaven, it probably looks a lot like this giant go-to store for manga and anime. Eight storeys are piled high with comic books, action

Tokyo Dome City

Tokyo Dome (東京ドーム; Map p134, C1; www.tokyo-dome.co.jp; 1-3 Kōraku, Bunkyō-ku; tickets ¥1700-6200; 🚉JR Chūō line to Suidōbashi, west exit), aka 'Big Egg', is home to the Yomiuri Giants, the most consistently successful team in Japanese baseball. If you're looking to see the Giants in action, the baseball season runs from the end of March to the end of October. Tickets sell out in advance; get them early at www.giants.jp.

The top attraction of the **amusement park** (東京ドームシティアトラクションズ; Map p134, C1; 📞03-5800-9999; www.tokyo-dome.co.jp; 1-3-61 Kōraku, Bunkyō-ku; day pass adult/child/teenager ¥3900/2500/3400; ⏰10am-9pm; 👶; 🚉JR Chūō line to Suidōbashi, west exit) next to Tokyo Dome is the 'Thunder Dolphin' (¥1030), a roller coaster that cuts a heart-in-your-throat course in and around the tightly packed buildings of downtown.

figures, *cosplay* accessories and cel art just for starters. The 1st floor has cases of some (very expensive) vintage toys. (まんだらけ コンプレックス; ☏03-3252-7007; www.mandarake.co.jp; 3-11-12 Soto-Kanda, Chiyoda-ku; ◷noon-8pm; ☒JR Yamanote line to Akihabara, Electric Town exit)

Y. & Sons
FASHION & ACCESSORIES

13 🔒 MAP P134, E2

Every once in a while in Tokyo, you'll spot a gentleman in a silk-wool kimono and a fedora, looking as if he's stepped out of the 1900s. Bespoke tailor Y. & Sons would like to see this more often. Custom kimonos with obi (sash) start at around ¥65,000 and take two weeks to complete; international shipping is available. (☏03-5294-7521; www.yandsons.com; 2-17-2 Soto-Kanda, Chiyoda-ku; ◷11am-8pm Thu-Tue; ☒JR Chūō line to Ochanomizu, Ochanomizu-bashi exit)

Onsen: Spa LaQua

One of Tokyo's few true onsen, chic **Spa LaQua** (スパ ラクーア; Map p134, C1; ☏03-5800-9999; www.laqua.jp; 5th-9th fl, Tokyo Dome City, 1-1-1 Kasuga, Bunkyō-ku; weekday/weekend ¥2850/3174; ◷11am-9am; ⑤Marunouchi line to Kōrakuen, exit 2) relies on natural hot-spring water from 1700m below ground. There are indoor and outdoor baths, saunas and a bunch of add-on options, such as *akasuri* (Korean-style whole-body exfoliation). It's a fascinating introduction to Japanese health and beauty rituals.

Explore ✦

Ueno & Yanesen

Ueno's central park, Ueno-kōen, has the city's highest concentration of museums, including the Tokyo National Museum. The neighbouring areas of Yanaka, Nezu and Sendagi are collectively known as Yanesen. It's a charming part of Tokyo that feels like time stopped several decades ago.

The Short List

○ **Tokyo National Museum (p142)** *Admire the finest collection of Japanese art and cultural artefacts in the world.*

○ **Ueno-kōen (p148)** *Enjoy this expansive park chock-a-block with museums, temples and even a zoo.*

○ **Nezu-jinja (p147)** *Visit this picturesque shrine with a corridor of mini red torii (gates) and azalea bushes.*

○ **Ameya-yokochō (p151)** *Shop in an old-fashioned partially outdoor market near Ueno station.*

○ **Ueno Tōshō-gū (p148)** *Recently restored, gilded homage to warlord that put Tokyo on the map, Tokugawa Ieyasu.*

Getting There & Around

🚃 JR trains stops at Ueno and Nippori (for Yanaka). Keisei trains from Narita Airport stop at Keisei Ueno Station.

Ⓢ The Ginza and Hibiya lines stop at Ueno. The Chiyoda line stops at Nezu and Sendagi, both convenient for Yanaka.

Neighbourhood Map on p146

Ameya-yokochō (p151) JON CHICA / SHUTTERSTOCK ©

Top Experience 📸
Admire art at Tokyo National Museum

If you visit only one museum in Tokyo, make it the Tokyo National Museum (東京国立博物館; Tokyo Kokuritsu Hakubutsukan). Established in 1872, this unprecedented collection of Japanese art covers ancient pottery, Buddhist sculpture, samurai swords, colourful ukiyo-e (woodblock prints), gorgeous kimonos and much, much more.

◎ MAP P146, D3

📞 03-3822-1111;
www.tnm.jp

13-9 Ueno-kōen, Taitō-ku

adult/child ¥620/free

🕘 9.30am-5pm Tue-Thu, to 9pm Fri & Sat, to 6pm Sun

🚇 JR lines to Ueno, Ueno-kōen exit

Honkan

The museum is divided into several buildings, the most important of which is the Honkan (Japanese Gallery), which houses the main collection. If you only have an hour or two, this is where you should spend it. The building itself is in the Imperial Style of the 1930s, with art deco flourishes throughout inside.

Gallery of Horyu-ji Treasures

Next visit the enchanting **Gallery of Hōryū-ji Treasures** (法隆寺宝物館; ☏03-5777-8600), which displays masks, scrolls and gilt Buddhas from Hōryū-ji (in Nara Prefecture, dating from 607) in an elegant, box-shaped contemporary building (1999) by Taniguchi Yoshio. Nearby, to the west of the main gate, is the **Kuro-mon** (黒門; Black Gate), transported from the Edo-era mansion of a feudal lord. On weekends it opens for visitors to pass through.

Toyōkan

Visitors with more time can explore the three-storeyed **Tōyōkan** (Gallery of Asian Art), with its collection of Asian artworks, including delicate Chinese ceramics, as well as a theatre screening short documentaries on historical art subjects.

Heiseikan

The **Heiseikan** (平成館), which can be accessed via a passage on the 1st floor of the Honkan, houses the Japanese Archaeological Gallery as well as temporary exhibitions (which cost extra); these can be fantastic, but sometimes lack the English signage found throughout the rest of the museum.

Also only used for special exhibitions and events is the 1909-vintage **Hyokeikan** (表慶館).

★ Top Tips

○ Allow two hours to take in the highlights, a half-day to do the Honkan in-depth or most of the day to take in everything.

○ Start with the 2nd floor of the Honkan and be sure to pick up the brochure *Highlights of Japanese Art* from room 1-1.

○ Exhibits rotate to protect works and present seasonal displays, so there's no guarantee that a particular work will be on display.

○ For a couple of weeks in spring and autumn, the back garden, home to five vintage teahouses, opens to the public; at other times there's a view from the 1st-floor terrace of the Honkan.

✕ Take a Break

The charming teahouse **Torindō** (桃林堂; ☏03-3828-9826; 1-5-7 Ueno-Sakuragi, Taitō-ku; ◷9.30am-5pm Tue-Sun; Ⓢ Chiyoda line to Nezu, exit 1) is a five-minute walk northwest of the museum.

Walking Tour 🥾

Yanaka

Much of Yanaka survived the ravages of the 20th century so you'll find a high concentration of vintage wooden structures here, as well as over a hundred temples and shrines. Many artists and craftspeople live and work in the neighbourhood. It's a fantastic place to spend a day wandering and is popular with Tokyoites, too, so can get crowded on weekends.

Walk Facts

Start Shitamachi Museum Annex; Ⓢ Chiyoda line to Nezu Station, exit 1

End Yanaka Ginza; JR Yamanote line to Nippori, north exit

Length 3km; two hours

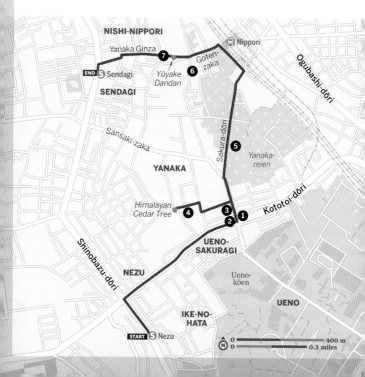

❶ Shitamachi Museum Annex

This century-old liquor shop (which operated until 1986) has been returned to its original state, but as a **museum** (下町風俗資料館; 📞03-3823-7451; www.taitocity.net/zaidan/shitamachi; 2-10-6 Ueno-sakuragi, Taitō-ku; admission free; 🕙9.30am-4.30pm Tue-Sun) of bygone Tokyo, with old sake barrels, weights, measures and posters.

❷ Kayaba Coffee

This vintage **coffee shop** (カヤバ珈琲; 📞03-3823-3545; http://kayaba-coffee.com; 6-1-29 Yanaka, Taitō-ku; coffee ¥450; 🕙8am-9pm Mon-Sat, to 6pm Sun), occupying a 1920s building, is a hang-out for local students and artists. It morphs into a bar in the evenings.

❸ SCAI

Nearby **SCAI the Bathhouse** (スカイザバスハウス; 📞03-3821-1144; www.scaithebathhouse.com; 6-1-23 Yanaka, Taitō-ku; admission free; 🕙noon-6pm Tue-Sat) is a classic old public bathhouse turned into an avant-garde gallery space, showcasing Japanese and international artists.

❹ Art Sanctuary Allan West

A skilfully converted garaged houses the studio of **Allan West** (繪処アラン・ウエスト; 📞03-3827-1907; www.allanwest.jp; 1-6-17 Yanaka, Taitō-ku; admission free; 🕙1.30-4.30pm Mon-Wed, Fri & Sat, from 3pm Sun), who paints gorgeous screens and scrolls in the traditional Japanese style, making his paints from scratch just as local artists have done for centuries. Look out nearby for the ancient, thick-trunked Himalayan cedar tree.

❺ Yanaka Cemetery

Yanaka-reien (谷中霊園; 📞03-3821-4456; www.tokyo-park.or.jp/reien; 7-5-24 Yanaka, Taitō-ku) is one of Tokyo's most atmospheric and prestigious cemeteries. Exit the cemetery, continue with the train tracks on your right, climbing until you reach the bridge, which overlooks the tracks (a favourite destination for trainspotters).

❻ Asakura Museum of Sculpture

Head left and look for the sign pointing towards the Asakura Museum of Sculpture (p147), the home studio of an early-20th-century sculptor and now an attractive museum.

❼ Yanaka Ginza

Continue down the **Yūyake Dandan** – literally the 'Sunset Stairs' – to the classic mid-20th-century shopping street **Yanaka Ginza** (谷中銀座; www.yanakaginza.com). Pick up some snacks from the vendors here, then hunker down on a milk crate on the side of the road with the locals and wash it all down with a beer.

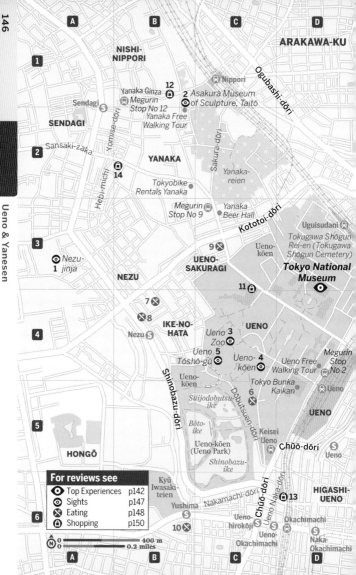

ARAKAWA-KU

NISHI-
NIPPORI

Nippori

Sendagi

Yanaka Ginza
Megurin
Stop No 12
Yanaka Free
Walking Tour

12

2 Asakura Museum
of Sculpture, Taitō

Ogubashi-dōri

SENDAGI

Sansaki-zaka

Yomise-dōri

Hebi-michi

14

YANAKA

Tokyobike
Rentals Yanaka

Sakura-dōri

Yanaka-
reien

Megurin
Stop No 9

Yanaka
Beer Hall

Kototoi-dōri

Uguisudani

Tokugawa Shōgun
Rei-en (Tokugawa
Shōgun Cemetery)

9

Ueno-
kōen

Nezu-
jinja

1

NEZU

UENO-
SAKURAGI

11

**Tokyo National
Museum**

7

8

Nezu

IKE-NO-
HATA

Ueno **3**
Zoo

UENO

Ueno
Tōshō-gū

5

Ueno- **4**
kōen

Ueno Free
Walking Tour

Megurin
Stop
No 2

Ueno

Shinobazu-dōri

Tokyo Bunka
Kaikan

6

UENO

Suijodobutsu-
ike

Keisei
Ueno

Chūō-dōri

Ueno

Bōto-
ike

Dōbutsuen-dōri

HONGŌ

Ueno-kōen
(Ueno Park)

Shinobazu-
ike

Kyū
Iwasaki-
teien

Yushima

Nakamachi-dōri

Ueno-
hirokōji

13

Chūō-dōri

Ueno Nakadōri

HIGASHI-
UENO

Okachimachi

10

Ueno-
Okachimachi

Naka-
Okachimachi

For reviews see	
⊙ Top Experiences	p142
⊙ Sights	p147
⊗ Eating	p148
🔒 Shopping	p150

0 — 400 m
0 — 0.2 miles

Sights

Nezu-jinja

SHINTO SHRINE

1 MAP P146, A3

Not only is this one of Japan's oldest shrines, it is also easily the most beautiful in a district packed with attractive religious buildings. The vermilion and gold structure, which dates from the early 18th century, is one of the city's miraculous survivors and is offset by a long corridor of small red *torii* that makes for great photos. (根津神社; ☏03-3822-0753; www.nedujinja.or.jp; 1-28-9 Nezu, Bunkyō-ku; ☉6am-5pm; Ⓢ Chiyoda line to Nezu, exit 1)

Asakura Museum of Sculpture, Taitō

MUSEUM

2 MAP P146, B1

Sculptor Asakura Fumio (artist name Chōso; 1883–1964) designed this atmospheric house himself. It combined his original Japanese home and garden with a large studio that incorporated vaulted ceilings, a 'sunrise room' and a rooftop garden with wonderful neighbourhood views. It's now a reverential museum with many of the artist's signature realist works, mostly of people and cats, on display. (朝倉彫塑館; ☏03-3821-4549; www.taitocity.net/taito/asakura; 7-16-10 Yanaka, Taitō-ku; adult/child ¥500/250; ☉9.30am-4.30pm Tue, Wed & Fri-Sun; Ⓡ JR Yamanote line to Nippori, north exit)

Free Walking Tours

No advance booking or payment is required for the **Yanaka Free Walking Tour** (Map p146, B2; ☏03-6280-6710; www.tokyosgg.jp; 7-8-10 Yanaka, Taitō-ku; ☉10.30am & 1.30pm Sun; Ⓡ Yamanote line to Nippori, north exit) or the **Ueno Free Walking Tour** (Map p146, D4; ☏03-6280-6710; www.tokyosgg.jp; 7-47 Ueno-kōen, Taitō-ku; ☉10.30am & 1.30pm Wed, Fri & Sun; Ⓡ JR lines to Ueno, Ueno-kōen exit).

Ueno Zoo

ZOO

3 MAP P146, C4

Japan's oldest zoo, established in 1882, is home to animals from around the globe, but the biggest attractions are the giant pandas that arrived from China in 2011 – Rī Rī and Shin Shin. Following several disappointments, the two finally had a cub, Xiang Xiang, in 2017. There's also a whole area devoted to lemurs, which makes sense given Tokyoites' love of all things cute. (上野動物園, Ueno Dōbutsu-en; ☏03-3828-5171; www.tokyo-zoo.net; 9-83 Ueno-kōen, Taitō-ku; adult/child ¥600/free; ☉9.30am-5pm Tue-Sun; Ⓡ JR lines to Ueno, Ueno-kōen exit)

Tokyobike Rentals Yanaka 🚲

Around the corner from its main showroom, the hipster bicycle manufacturer **Tokyobike** (Map p146, B2; 📞03-5809-0980; www.tokyobikerentals.com; 4-2-39 Yanaka, Taitō-ku; 1st day ¥3000, additional day ¥1500; ⏰10am-7.30pm Wed-Mon; 🚃JR Yamanote line to Nippori, west exit) rents seven- and eight-speed city bikes for the day. Book ahead online. Helmet and locker rentals (¥500 each) are available too, and there's a good shop and pleasant cafe also serving craft beer here.

Ueno-kōen   PARK

4 ◉ MAP P146, C4

Best known for its profusion of cherry trees that burst into blossom in spring (making this one of Tokyo's top *hanami* – blossom-viewing – spots), sprawling Ueno-kōen is also the location of the city's highest concentration of museums. At the southern tip is the large scenic pond, **Shinobazu-ike** (不忍池; Ueno-kōen, Taitō-ku; Ⓢ JR lines to Ueno, Shinobazu exit), choked with lotus flowers in summer. (上野公園; www.ueno-bunka.jp; Ueno-kōen, Taitō-ku; 🚃JR lines to Ueno, Ueno-kōen & Shinobazu exits)

Ueno Tōshō-gū   SHINTO SHRINE

5 ◉ MAP P146, C4

This shrine inside Ueno-kōen was built in honour of Tokugawa Ieyasu, the warlord who unified Japan. Resplendent in gold leaf and ornate details, it dates from 1651 (though it has had recent touch-ups). You can look from outside the gate, if you want to skip the admission fee.

In January and February there is a spectacular peony garden; from mid-September to 30 October it blooms with dahlias. Entry to either is an additional ¥700. (上野東照宮; 📞03-3822-3455; www.uenotoshogu.com; 9-88 Ueno-kōen, Taitō-ku; adult/child ¥500/200; ⏰9am-5.30pm Mar-Sep, to 4.30pm Oct-Feb; 🚃JR lines to Ueno, Shinobazu exit)

Eating

Innsyoutei   JAPANESE ¥

6 🍴 MAP P146, C5

In a gorgeous wooden building dating back to 1875, Innsyoutei (pronounced 'inshotei' and meaning 'rhyme of the pine cottage') has long been a favourite spot for fancy *kaiseki*-style (Japanse haute cuisine) meals while visiting Ueno-kōen. Without a booking (essential for dinner) you'll have a long wait but it's worth it. Lunchtime *bentō* (boxed meals) offer beautifully presented morsels and are great value. (韻松亭; 📞03-3821-8126; www.innsyoutei.jp; 4-59 Ueno-kōen, Taitō-ku; lunch/dinner from ¥1680/5500;

SEAN PAVONE / SHUTTERSTOCK ©

Ueno Tōshō-gū

restaurant 11am-3pm & 5-9.30pm;
JR lines to Ueno, Ueno-kōen exit)

Kamachiku UDON ¥

7 MAP P146, B4

Freshly made udon (thick wheat noodles) are the speciality at this popular restaurant, in a beautifully restored brick warehouse from 1910 that's incorporated into a building designed by Kengo Kuma. In addition to noodles, the menu includes a good selection of sake and lots of small dishes such as grilled fish, veggies and a delicious Japanese-style omelette. (釜竹; 03-5815-4675; www.kamachiku.com; 2-14-18 Nezu, Bunkyō-ku; noodles from ¥850, small dishes ¥350-950; 11.30am-2pm Tue-Sun, 5.30-9pm Tue-Sat; Chiyoda line to Nezu, exit 1)

Hantei JAPANESE ¥¥

8 MAP P146, B4

Housed in a beautifully maintained, century-old traditional wooden building, Hantei is a local landmark. Delectable skewers of seasonal *kushiage* (fried meat, fish and vegetables) are served with small, refreshing side dishes. Lunch includes eight or 12 sticks and dinner starts with six, after which you can order additional rounds (three/six skewers ¥800/1600). (はん亭; 03-3287-9000; www.hantei.co.jp; 2-12-15 Nezu, Bunkyō-ku; lunch/dinner from ¥3200/3000; noon-3pm & 5-10pm Tue-Sun; Chiyoda line to Nezu, exit 2)

Yanaka Beer Hall

Exploring Yanesen can be thirsty work so thank heavens for this craft-beer **bar** (谷中ビアホール; Map p146, C3; ☏03-5834-2381; www.facebook.com/yanakabeerhall; 2-15-6 Ueno-sakuragi, Taitō-ku; ☉noon-8.30pm Tue-Fri, from 11am Sat & Sun; Ⓢ Chiyoda line to Nezu, exit 1), a cosy place with some outdoor seating. It's part of a charming complex of old wooden buildings that also house a bakery-cafe, a bistro and an events space. It has several brews on tap, including a Yanaka lager (¥970) that's only available here.

Ueno-Sakuragi Nanohana

JAPANESE ¥¥

9 ⊗ MAP P146, C3

The family who run this charming little restaurant source many of their organic ingredients, including the rice, pickles and vegetables for side dishes, from the chef's mother who lives on Sado-ga-shima. The house speciality is *ochazuke* – rice mixed with cuts of raw fish, other toppings and a clear broth. (上野桜木 菜の花; ☏03-3827-3511; 1-10-26 Ueno-Sakuragi, Taitō-ku; lunch/dinner ¥1580/5400; ☉11am-2pm & 5.30-9.30pm Tue-Sat, 11am-4pm Sun; Ⓢ Chiyoda line to Nezu, exit 1)

Shinsuke

IZAKAYA ¥¥

10 ⊗ MAP P146, B6

In business since 1925, Shinsuke has honed the concept of an ideal *izakaya* (Japanese pub eatery) to perfection: long cedar counter, 'master' in *happi* (traditional short coat) and *hachimaki* (traditional headband), and smooth-as-silk *daiginjō* (premium-grade sake). The menu, updated monthly, includes house specialities (such as *kitsune raclette* – deep-fried tofu stuffed with raclette cheese) and seasonal dishes; note portions are small. Reservations are recommended. (シンスケ; ☏03-3832-0469; 3-31-5 Yushima, Bunkyō-ku; dishes ¥500-2500, cover charge ¥300; ☉5-9.30pm Mon-Fri, to 9pm Sat; Ⓢ Chiyoda line to Yushima, exit 3)

Shopping

Geidai Art Plaza

ARTS & CRAFTS

11 🔒 MAP P146, C3

On the campus of Tokyo's top arts university, this shop, opened in 2018, showcases creative pieces in a range of media by the institute's staff, students and graduates. It's well worth a browse, and if you can't afford an original work there are plenty of affordable things too, including books, comics and specially designed biscuits. (☏050-5525-2102; www.artplaza.geidai.ac.jp; Tokyo University of the Arts, 12-8 Ueno-kōen, Taitō-ku; ☉10am-6pm Tue-Sun; 🚃 JR lines to Ueno, Ueno-kōen exit)

Yanaka Matsunoya HOMEWARES

12 🔒 MAP P146, B1

At the top of Yanaka Ginza (p145), Matsunoya sets out its stall with an attractive range of mainly household goods – baskets, brooms and canvas totes, for example – simple in beauty and form, and handmade by local artisans. (谷中松野屋; ☎03-3823-7441; www.yanakamatsunoya.jp; 3-14-14 Nishi-Nippori, Arakawa-ku; ⏰11am-7pm Mon & Wed-Fri, from 10am Sat & Sun; 🚇JR Yamanote line to Nippori, west exit)

Ameya-yokochō MARKET

13 🔒 MAP P146, D6

Step into this partially open-air market paralleling and beneath the JR line tracks, and ritzy, glitzy Tokyo feels like a distant memory. It got its start as a black market, post-WWII, when American goods (which included *ameya* – candy and chocolates) were sold here. Today you can pick up everything from fresh seafood to vintage jeans and bargain sneakers. (アメヤ横町; www.ameyoko.net; 4 Ueno, Taitō-ku; ⏰10am-7pm, some shops close Wed; 🚇JR lines to Okachi-machi, north exit)

Classical Concerts

The Tokyo Metropolitan Symphony Orchestra and the Tokyo Ballet both make regular appearances at **Tokyo Bunka Kaikan** (東京文化会館; Map p146, D5; ☎03-3828-2111; www.t-bunka.jp; 5-45 Ueno-kōen, Taitō-ku; ⏰library 1-8pm Tue-Sat, to 5pm Sun, closed irregularly; 🚇JR lines to Ueno, Ueno-kōen exit), a building designed by Maekawa Kunio, an apprentice of Le Corbusier. Prices vary wildly; look out for monthly morning classical-music performances that cost only ¥500. The gorgeously decorated auditorium, with cloud-shaped acoustic panels on the wall, has superb acoustics.

Isetatsu ARTS & CRAFTS

14 🔒 MAP P146, B2

Dating back to 1864, this venerable stationery shop specialises in *chiyogami* – gorgeous, colourful paper made using woodblocks – as well as papier-mâché figures and masks. (いせ辰; ☎03-3823-1453; www.isetatsu.com; 2-18-9 Yanaka, Taitō-ku; ⏰10am-6pm; Ⓢ Chiyoda line to Sendagi, exit 1)

Top Experience 📷
Take a stroll through Rikugi-en

Considered by many to be Tokyo's most elegant garden, Rikugi-en (六義園) was originally completed in 1702, at the behest of a feudal lord. It is definitely the most highbrow, designed to evoke scenes from classical literature and mythology. But no context is necessary to appreciate the wooded walkways, stone bridges, central pond, trickling streams and wooden teahouses of this beautifully preserved garden.

http://teien.tokyo-park.
or.jp/en/rikugien

6-16-3 Hon-Komagome,
Bunkyō-ku

adult/child/senior ¥300/
free/150; ⊙9am-5pm

S Namboku line to Koma-
gome, exit 2

🚆 JR train to Komagome

Poetic Views

Rikugi-en is a classic example of an Edo-era strolling garden. Such gardens are designed as a series of sensory encounters (often visual, but they can be auditory too – rushing water, for example) that unfold along a meandering path. It's one of only three that remain in Tokyo, but centuries ago they were all the rage among the feudal elite.

There are 88 viewpoints that evoke scenes from poetry and legend or recreate (in miniature) famous vistas found in Japan and China. One example is the bridge, **Togetsukyō**, created from two huge stone slabs, that references a poem about a crane flying over a moonlit field. Another is the craggy rock in the pond, called **Hōrai-jima**, which represents the Taoist 'Isle of Immortals'.

Stone markers around the garden make note of other scenic viewpoints (even the most erudite Japanese visitor wouldn't get them all); some are signposted with English explanations as well.

Teahouses

Rikugi-en has two vintage teahouses: **Tsutsuji-chaya** dates to the Meiji period and is perfectly primed for viewing the maples in autumn. **Takimi-chaya** is perched on the edge of the stream where you can enjoy the view of a mini waterfall over rocks and giant koi (carp) swimming in the water.

Seasonal Blooms

Something is almost always in bloom at Rikugi-en. The garden is most famous for its maple leaves, which turn bright red usually around late November and early December. During this time, the park stays open until 9pm and the trees are illuminated after sunset. In early spring you can catch plum blossoms, followed by the flowering of the magnificent weeping cherry tree near the entrance.

★ Top Tips

○ Climb to the top of the **Fujishiro-tōge**, a hill named after the real one in Wakayama Prefecture, for panoramic views across the garden.

○ Free, hour-long guided tours in English are offered at 11am and 2pm on the 1st and 3rd Sunday of the month.

○ Even in winter the gardens are worth visiting to note interesting features such as the ropes strung from the pruned pine trees, which protect their branches from heavy snowfall.

✗ Take a Break

Inside Rikugi-en, **Fukiage-chaya** is not an antique teahouse but is attractive and provides a beautiful view of the central pond as you sip *matcha* (powered green tea; ¥510) and enjoy a seasonal *wagashi* (sweet).

Explore ◎

Asakusa, Ryōgoku & Sumida River

Tokyo's eastern neighbourhoods, on the banks of the Sumida-gawa, have an old-Tokyo (Shitamachi) feel, with venerable temples and shrines, lovely gardens, traditional restaurants and artisan shops. Zone in on Asakusa's atmospheric Buddhist temple complex Sensō-ji and the sumo hotspot of Ryōgoku, home to the ancient sport's Tokyo stadium and a top-class history museum.

The Short List

○ **Sensō-ji (p156)** Approach the centuries-old temple complex via the craft stalls of Nakamise-dōri.

○ **Ryōgoku Kokugikan (p158)** Book your ticket for this hallowed hall of sumo tournaments.

○ **Edo-Tokyo Museum (p164)** Step into the past at this top museum focused on Tokyo's history.

○ **Tokyo Skytree (p165)** Look out from the world's tallest communication tower.

○ **Fukagawa Fudō-dō (p171)** Visit this shingon-sect temple with spectacular fire ritual.

Getting There & Around

🚊 The Tōbu Skytree line leaves from Tōbu Asakusa Station for Tokyo Skytree Station. The JR Sōbu line goes to Ryōgoku.

Ⓢ The Ginza line stops at Asakusa. The Asakusa line stops at a separate Asakusa Station and at Oshiage. The Ōedo and Hanzōmon lines connect across to stations on the east side of the Sumida River.

Neighbourhood Map on p162

Sensō-ji (p156) 501ROOM / SHUTTERSTOCK ©

Top Experience 📷
Soak up the atmosphere at Sensō-ji

Sensō-ji is the capital's oldest temple, far older than Tokyo itself. According to legend, in AD 628 two fishermen brothers pulled out a golden image of Kannon (the Bodhisattva of compassion) from the nearby Sumida-gawa. Sensō-ji (浅草寺)was built to enshrine it. Today the temple stands out for its atmosphere of an older Japan, rarely visible in Tokyo today.

◎ MAP P162, C2

☎ 03-3842-0181

www.senso-ji.jp

2-3-1 Asakusa, Taitō-ku

admission free

🕒 24hr

Ⓢ Ginza line to Asakusa, exit 1

Kaminari-mon

The temple precinct begins at the majestic Kaminari-mon, which means Thunder Gate. An enormous *chōchin* (lantern) hangs from the centre. On either side are a pair of ferocious protective deities: Fūjin, the god of wind, on the right; and Raijin, the god of thunder, on the left. Kaminari-mon has burnt down countless times over the centuries; the current gate dates to 1970.

Nakamise-dōri Shopping Street

The bustling shopping street Nakamise-dōri lined with souvenir stands, is very touristy, though that's nothing new: Sensō-ji has been a top Tokyo attraction for centuries, since travel was restricted to religious pilgrimages during the feudal era. Look out for Edo-style crafts and numerous snack vendors serving crunchy *sembei* (rice crackers) and *age-manju* (deep-fried *anko* – bean-paste – buns).

At the end of Nakamise-dōri is **Hōzō-mon**, another gate with fierce guardians. On the gate's back side are a pair of 2500kg, 4.5m-tall *waraji* (straw sandals). These are meant to symbolise the Buddha's power, and it's believed that evil spirits will be scared off by the giant footwear.

Main Hall

In front of the grand **Hondō** (Main Hall), with its dramatic sloping roof, is a large cauldron with smoking incense. The smoke is said to bestow health and you'll see people wafting it over their bodies. The current Hondō was constructed in 1958, replacing the one destroyed in WWII air raids.

The **Kannon image** (a tiny 6cm) is cloistered away from view deep inside the Main Hall and admittedly may not exist at all. Nonetheless, a steady stream of worshippers visit the temple to cast coins, pray and bow in a gesture of respect. Do feel free to join in.

★ **Top Tips**

o The Main Hall and its gates are illuminated every day from sunset until 11pm. The minutes just before the sun sinks make for some of the best pictures of this photogenic sanctuary.

o Consider the crowds part of the experience, as there doesn't seem to be a time of day when Sensō-ji isn't packed, though there are usually fewer people at night.

✕ **Take a Break**

Just off Nakamise-dōri, **Daikokuya** (大黒家; ☎03-3844-1111; www.tempura. co.jp; 1-38-10 Asakusa, Taitō-ku; meals ¥1550-2100; ⊙11am-8.30pm Sun-Fri, to 9pm Sat; Ⓢ Ginza line to Asakusa, exit 1) serves delicious tempura in an unpretentious setting that is typical of Asakusa.

Asakusa, Ryōgoku & Sumida River Soak up the atmosphere at Sensō-ji

Top Experience 📷

Catch a sumo bout at Ryōgoku Kokugikan

Travellers visiting Tokyo in January, May or September should not miss the opportunity to attend one of the 15-day sumo tournaments at the national stadium, Ryōgoku Kokugikan. Never mind if you're a sports fan or not, ancient sumo is just as captivating for its spectacle and ritual. During the rest of the year, catch the action at one of the neighbourhood stables.

◉ MAP P162, B8

両国国技館
Ryōgoku Sumo Stadium

📞 03-3623-5111

www.sumo.or.jp

1-3-28 Yokoami, Sumida-ku

tickets ¥3800-11,700t

The Ritual of Sumo

Sumo was originally part of a ritual prayer to the gods for a good harvest. While it has obviously evolved, it remains deeply connected to Japan's Shintō tradition. You'll see a roof suspended over the *dōyo* (ring) that resembles that of a shrine. Before bouts, *rikishi* (wrestlers) rinse their mouths with water and toss salt into the ring – both are purification rituals.

Rising Through the Ranks

Doors open at 8am, with the first matches fought by lower ranking wrestlers. The pageantry (and the stakes) begin in earnest in the afternoon, when the *makuuchi* (top-tier) wrestlers perform their ceremonial entrance, followed by that of the *yokozuna* (the top of the top) complete with sword-bearing attendants.

In order to achieve this highest rank a wrestler must win two consecutive tournaments and be considered, in the eyes of the Sumo Association, to embody certain traditional values. While sumo is very Japanese in origin, in fact many of the top wrestlers are foreign-born (Mongolia is a sumo powerhouse). The *yokozuna* wrestle in the final, most exciting, bouts of the day. You'll also see portraits of past champions hanging around the stadium and at the **Sumo Museum** attached to the stadium.

Sumo Practice

If you're not visiting during a tournament, you can watch an early-morning practice at **Arashio Stable** (荒汐部屋, Arashio-beya; ☎03-3666-7646; www.arashio.net; 2-47-2 Hama-chō, Nihombashi, Chūō-ku; admission free; ⏰7.30am-10am; ⑤Toei Shinjuku line to Hamachō, exit A2), one of several stables where wrestlers sleep, eat and train. See the website for information on visiting and etiquette.

★ Top Tips

o Reserved seats range between ¥3800 and ¥14,800. Same-day unreserved seats can be bought from the stadium box office for only ¥2200.

o On the last days of the tournament, get in line by 6am to score a same-day ticket.

o You can rent a radio (¥100 fee, plus ¥2000 deposit) to listen to commentary in English.

✕ Take a Break

Stop by the basement banquet hall to sample *chanko-nabe* (the protein-rich stew eaten by the wrestlers) for just ¥300 a bowl.

★ Getting There

Train Take the JR Sōbu line to Ryōgoku and use the west exit; the stadium is a two-minute walk away.

Subway The Ōedo line also stops at Ryōgoku.

Walking Tour 🥾

Shitamachi

This walk takes in the major sights in Asakusa, while giving you a feel for the flavour of Shitamachi – the old Edo-era 'Low City' where merchants and artisans lived during the Edo period (1603–1868). It's almost always busy around Sensō-ji, but step off the main drags and you'll find far fewer tourists, and the craft shops and small restaurants that have long defined these quarters.

Walk Facts

Start Azuma-bashi; Ⓢ Asakusa Station, exit 4

End Ef; Ⓢ Asakusa Station, exit 2

Length 2.5km; 2½ hours, plus lunch

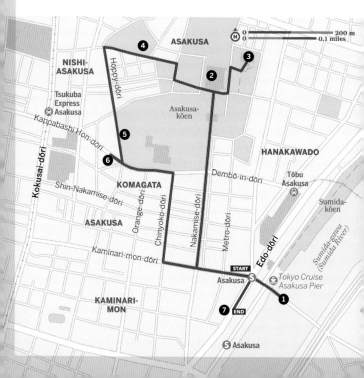

❶ Azuma-bashi

Originally built in 1774, **Azuma-bashi** (吾妻橋; 2 Kaminari-mon, Taitō-ku) was once the point of departure for boat trips to the Yoshiwara pleasure district, north of Asakusa. From here you can get a good look at the golden flame of Asahi Super Dry Hall and the giant Tokyo Skytree, both across the river.

❷ Sensō-ji

Make your way to **Kaminari-mon**, the entrance to the grand temple complex Sensō-ji (p156). Spend some time exploring Tokyo's oldest and most atmospheric place of Buddhist worship.

❸ Asakusa-jinja

Asakusa-jinja (浅草神社; ☎03-3844-1575; www.asakusajinja.jp; 2-3-1 Asakusa, Taitō-ku; ⊙9am-4.30pm) was built in honour of the brothers who discovered the Kannon statue that inspired the construction of Sensō-ji. The current building, painted a deep shade of red, dates to 1649 and is a rare example of early Edo architecture.

❹ Hanayashiki

Japan's oldest amusement **park** (花やしき; ☎03-3842-8780; www.hanayashiki.net/index.html; 2-28-1 Asakusa, Taitō-ku; adult/child ¥1000/500; ⊙10am-6pm) opened originally as a flower park in 1853. It offers creaky old carnival rides and heaps of vintage charm.

❺ Hoppy-dōri

Along either side of the street popularly known as **Hoppy-dōri** (ホッピー通り; 2-5 Asakusa, Taitō-ku; dishes ¥500-700; ⊙noon until late, varies by shop) – 'hoppy' is a cheap malt beverage – are rows of *izakaya* (pub eatery) with outdoor seating on rickety stools and plastic tarps for awnings – it's one of Asakusa's most atmospheric eating and drinking strips.

❻ Tokyo Hotarudo

Pay a visit to vintage store **Tokyo Hotarudo** (東京蛍堂; ☎03-3845-7563; http://tokyohotarudo.com; 1-41-8 Asakusa, Taitō-ku; ⊙11am-8pm Wed-Sun), where the goods pay homage to the early 20th century, when Asakusa was thought of as the Montmartre of Tokyo.

❼ Ef

Having navigated your way past the craft and souvenir stalls of Nakamise-dōri, finish up at **Ef** (エフ; ☎03-3841-0442; www.gallery-ef.com; 2-19-18 Kaminari-mon, Taitō-ku; ⊙11am-midnight Mon, Wed, Thu & Sat, to 2am Fri, to 10pm Sun), a cafe-bar in a 19th-century wooden warehouse.

Asakusa, Ryōgoku & Sumida River

0.2 miles

400 m

HIGASHI-MUKŌJIMA

OSHIAGE

Tokyo Sky Tree Station

Skytree 4

NARIHIRA

MUKŌJIMA

Mitsume-dōri

Kototoi-bashi

Sumida-kōen

IMADO

Sumida-kōen

Yoshino-dōri

Tokyo Mizube Cruising Line Niten-mon Pier

Shuto Expwy No 6

Sumida-kōen

AZUMABASHI

Honjo-Azumabashi

HIGASHI-

Asahi Super Dry Hall

Tokyo Cruise Asakusa Pier

Tōbu Asakusa

11

Metro-dōri

Umamichi-dōri

Edo-dōri

HANAKAWADO

Amuse Museum 2

Senso-ji ◉

Kototoi-dōri

ASAKUSA

Asakusa-kōen

Chōchin Monaka 21

Dembo-in-dōri

17

Asakusa Free Walking Tour

Azuma-bashi

Asakusa

Komagata-bashi

Nakamise-dōri

Hanayashiki Amusement Park

9

Hisago-dōri

Hoppy-dōri

15

Sushiya-dōri

KOMAGATA

20

Shin-Nakamise-dōri

Mokuhankan 7

Asakusa Culture Tourist Information Center

Dembōn-dōri

Wanariya

6

18

NISHI-ASAKUSA

16

Ganso Shokuhin Sample-ya

Kappabashi Hon-dōri

Kama-asa

Tsukuba Express Asakusa

13

Tsukuba

Kappabashi-dōri

Soi

8 ASAKUSA

Kaminari-mon-dōri

KAMINARI-MON

10

Asakusa-dōri

KOMAGATA

Tawaramachi

KOTOBUKI

Kasuga-dōri

Kuramaebashi-dōri

Kasuga-dōri

Kuramaebashi-dōri

Kokusai-dōri

KURAMAE

YOKOAMI

SUMIDA-KU

RYŌGOKU

Ⓢ Kuramae

Ⓢ Kuramae

Ⓢ Kuramae

Ⓢ Asakusabashi

Kuramae-bashi

Ⓧ 12

5 Sumida Hokusai Museum

Ⓢ Ryōgoku

Yokoami-kōen

Edo-Tokyo Museum Ⓞ 1

Ⓢ Ryōgoku

Former Yasuda Garden

Tokyo Mizube Cruising Line Ryōgoku Pier

Ryōgoku Kokugikan Ⓞ

Sumida-gawa (Sumida River)

Ryōgoku

Ⓞ 14

Sights

Edo-Tokyo Museum
MUSEUM

1 ◉ MAP P162, C8

Tokyo's history museum documents the city's transformation from tidal flatlands to feudal capital to modern metropolis via detailed scale recreations of townscapes, villas and tenement homes, plus artefacts such as *ukiyo-e* (woodblock prints) and old maps. Reopened in March 2018 after a renovation, the museum also has interactive displays, multilingual touch-screen panels and audio guides. Still, the best way to tour the museum is with one of the gracious English-speaking volunteer guides, who can really bring the history to life. (江戸東京博物館;

☎03-3626-9974; www.edo-tokyo-museum.or.jp; 1-4-1 Yokoami, Sumida-ku; adult/child ¥600/free; ◷9.30am-5.30pm, to 7.30pm Sat, closed Mon; ◻JR Sōbu line to Ryōgoku, west exit)

Amuse Museum
MUSEUM

2 ◉ MAP P162, C2

The highlight of this museum is a fascinating collection of Japanese folk articles, mainly patched clothing and pieces of fabric, known as *boro,* gathered by famed ethnologist Tanaka Chūzaburō. Many of the pieces are like fine works of contemporary art. On another floor there's a video tutorial (with English subtitles) on how to find secret meaning in *ukiyo-e.* Don't miss the roof terrace, which looks over the Sensō-ji (p156) temple complex. (アミューズミュージアム;

Tokyo Skytree

📧 03-5806-1181; www.amusemuseum.com; 2-34-3 Asakusa, Taitō-ku; adult/child ¥1080/540; ⏰ 10am-6pm; Ⓢ Ginza line to Asakusa, exit 1)

Asahi Super Dry Hall ARCHITECTURE

3 ◉ MAP P162, D3

Also known as Asahi Beer Hall, the headquarters of the brewery – designed by Philippe Starck and completed in 1989 – remains one of Tokyo's most distinctive buildings. The tower, with its golden glass facade and white top floors, is supposed to evoke a giant mug of beer, while the golden blob atop the lower jet-black building is the flame – locals, however, refer to it as the 'golden turd'. (フラムドール, Flamme d'Or; 1-23-1 Azuma-bashi, Sumida-ku; Ⓢ Ginza line to Asakusa, exit 4)

Tokyo Skytree TOWER

4 ◉ MAP P162, F3

Tokyo Skytree opened in May 2012 as the world's tallest 'free-standing tower' at 634m. Its silvery exterior of steel mesh morphs from a triangle at the base to a circle at 300m. There are two observation decks, at 350m and 450m. You can see more of the city during daylight hours – at peak visibility you can see up to 100km away, all the way to Mt Fuji – but it is at night that Tokyo appears truly beautiful. (東京スカイツリー; 📧 0570-55-0102; www.tokyo-skytree.jp; 1-1-2 Oshiage, Sumida-ku; 350m/450m observation decks ¥2060/3090; ⏰ 8am-10pm; Ⓢ Hanzōmon line to Oshiage, Tokyo Skytree exit)

Water Buses ⛵

Tokyo Mizube Cruising Line

(東京水辺ライン; Map p162, D2; 📧 03-5608-8869; www.tokyo-park.or.jp/waterbus) water buses depart from Niten-mon Pier in Asakusa for Odaiba, via Ryōgoku. It's actually the most convenient way to get between Asakusa and Ryōgoku (¥310, one way 10 minutes) and is the perfect opportunity for travellers short on time to sample a river cruise.

Sumida Hokusai Museum MUSEUM

5 ◉ MAP P162, D8

The woodblock artist Katsushika Hokusai (1760–1849) was born and died close to the location of this museum, which opened in 2016 in a striking aluminium-clad building designed by Pritzker Prize–winning architect *Sejima Kazuyo*. The small permanent exhibition gives an overview of his life and work, mostly through replicas. (すみだ北斎美術館; 📧 03-5777-8600; http://hokusai-museum.jp; 2-7-2 Kamezawa, Sumida-ku; adult/child/student & senior ¥400/free/300; ⏰ 9.30am-5.30pm Tue-Sun; Ⓢ Oedo line to Ryōgoku, exit A4)

Wanariya TRADITIONAL CRAFT

6 ◉ MAP P162, A1

A team of young and friendly Japanese runs this indigo dyeing and traditional *hataori* (hand-loom-weaving) workshop. In under an hour you can learn to dye a T-shirt or a tote bag or weave a pair of coasters. Book at least three days in advance; solo travellers OK. (和なり屋; ☏03-5603-9169; www.wanariya.jp; 1-8-10 Senzoku, Taitō-ku; indigo dyeing/weaving from ¥1920/1980; ⏱10am-7pm, irregular holidays; Ⓢ Hibiya line to Iriya, exit 1)

Mokuhankan
TRADITIONAL CRAFT

7 ◉ MAP P162, B2

Try your hand at making *ukiyo-e* at this studio run by expat David Bull. Hour-long 'print parties' are great fun and take place daily; sign up online. There's a shop here too, where you can buy vintage prints as well as Bull's and Jed Henry's humorous *Ukiyo-e Heroes* series – contemporary

> **Views & Tours**
>
> The roof terrace of the **Asakusa Culture Tourist Information Center** (浅草文化観光センター; Map p162, C3; ☏03-3842-5566; www.city.taito.lg.jp; 2-18-9 Kaminari-mon, Taitō-ku; ⏱9am-8pm; 🛜; Ⓢ Ginza line to Asakusa, exit 2) has fantastic views of Tokyo Skytree and the Nakamise-dōri approach to Sensō-ji. Free guided **tours** (☏03-6280-6710; ⏱10.30am & 1.15pm Sat-Mon) of Asakusa depart from here, too.

prints featuring video-game characters in traditional settings. (木版館; ☏070-5011-1418; www.mokuhankan.com; 1-41-8 Asakusa, Taitō-ku; per person ¥2000; ⏱10am-5.30pm Wed-Mon; 🚆 Tsukuba Express to Asakusa, exit 5)

Eating

Misojyu
JAPANESE ¥

8 ✖ MAP P162, B3

The Japanese meal staples of rice, in the form of *onigiri* (rice balls), and miso soup are given a stylish update at Misojyu. All ingredients are organic and recipes range from traditional to contemporary, such as miso soup with beef and tomato, and brown rice *onigiri* covered in tea leaves. A limited breakfast menu is served until 11am. (☏03-5830-3101; www.misojyu.jp; 1-7-5 Asakusa, Taitō-ku; miso soup ¥780, set menu from ¥1280; ⏱8.30am-7pm Tue-Sun; 🚆 Tsukuba Express to Asakusa, exit 4)

Onigiri Yadoroku
JAPANESE ¥

9 ✖ MAP P162, B1

Onigiri wrapped in crispy sheets of *nori* (seaweed), are a great Japanese culinary invention. Try them freshly made at Tokyo's oldest *onigiri* shop, which feels more like a classy sushi counter. The set lunches are a great deal; at night there's a large range of flavours to choose from, along with alcohol. (おにぎり　浅草　宿六; ☏03-3874-1615; www.onigiriyadoroku.com; 3-9-10

Asakusa, Taitō-ku; set lunch 2/3 onigiri from ¥690/930, onigiri ¥280-690; ⏱11.30am-5pm Mon-Sat, 6pm-2am Thu-Tue; 🚇Tsukuba Express to Asakusa, exit 1)

Sometarō
OKONOMIYAKI ¥

10 🍴 MAP P162, A3

Sometarō is a fun and funky place to try *okonomiyaki* (savoury Japanese-style pancakes filled with meat, seafood and vegetables that you cook yourself). This historic, vine-covered house is a friendly spot where the menu includes a how-to guide for novice cooks. Tatami seating; cash only. (染太郎; 📞03-3844-9502; 2-2-2 Nishi-Asakusa, Taitō-ku; mains from ¥700; ⏱noon-10pm; S Ginza line to Tawaramachi, exit 3)

Otafuku
JAPANESE ¥¥

11 🍴 MAP P162, C3

In business for over a century, Otafuku specialises in *oden*, a classic Japanese hotpot dish of vegetables and seafood simmered in a soy sauce and *dashi* (fish stock) broth. You can dine cheaply on radishes and kelp, or splash out on scallops and tuna or a full-course menu for ¥5400. It's above the Daily Yamazaki convenience store. (大多福; 📞03-3871-2521; www.otafuku.ne.jp; 3rd fl, 1-2-6 Hanakawado, Taitō-ku; oden ¥100-500; ⏱11.30am-2pm & 5-11pm Tue-Fri, 4-11pm Sat, to 9pm Sun; 🚇Ginza line to Asakusa, exit 5)

Asakusa Street Food 🍴

Traditionally, monaka are wafers filled with sweet bean jam. At **Chōchin Monaka** (ちょうちんもなか; Map p162, C2; 2-3-1 Asakusa, Taitō-ku; ice cream ¥330; ⏱10am-5pm; S Ginza line to Asakusa, exit 1), a little stand on Nakamise-dōri, they're filled with ice cream instead – in flavours such as matcha (powdered green tea) and kuro-goma (black sesame).

Kappō Yoshiba
JAPANESE ¥¥

12 🍴 MAP P162, C6

The former Miyagino sumo stable is the location for this one-of-a-kind restaurant that has preserved the *dōyō* (practice ring) as its centrepiece. Playing up to its sumo roots, you can order the protein-packed stew *chanko-nabe* (for two people from ¥5200), but Yoshiba's real strength is its sushi, which is freshly prepared in jumbo portions. (割烹吉葉; 📞03-3623-4480; www.kapou-yoshiba.jp; 2-14-5 Yokoami, Sumida-ku; dishes ¥650-7800; ⏱11.30am-2pm & 5-10pm Mon-Sat; S Ōedo line to Ryōgoku, exit 1)

Asakusa Imahan
JAPANESE ¥¥¥

13 🍴 MAP P162, B2

For a meal to remember, swing by this famous beef restaurant, in business since 1895. Choose between courses of sukiyaki (sautéed beef dipped in raw egg) and *shabu-shabu* (beef blanched in broth); prices rise according to the grade of meat. (浅草今半; 📞03-3841-1114; www.asakusaimahan.co.jp; 3-1-12 Nishi-Asakusa, Taitō-ku; lunch/dinner from ¥2000/8000; ⏰11.30am-9.30pm; 🚇Tsukuba Express to Asakusa, exit 4

Drinking

Popeye
PUB

14 🚇 MAP P162, B8

Popeye boasts an astounding 100 beers on tap, including a huge selection of Japanese beers – from Echigo Weizen to Hitachino Nest Espresso Stout. Happy hour is from 5pm to 8pm, from 3pm on Saturday. It's extremely popular and fills up fast; get here early. (ポパイ; 📞03-3633-2120; www.lares.dti.ne.jp/~ppy; 2-18-7 Ryōgoku, Sumida-ku; sampler set of 3/10 beers ¥630/1750; ⏰5-11.30pm Mon-Fri, from 3pm Sat; 🚇JR Sōbu line to Ryōgoku, west exit)

Fuglen
COFFEE

15 🚇 MAP P162, B2

This Norwegian coffee and cocktail bar brings its oh-so-cool vintage Scandi stylings to Asakusa. The coffee is very good but it's also a sophisticated place to chill over delicious concoctions, such as a rum and maple marmalade cocktail. (📞03-5811-1756; www.fuglen.com; 2-6-15 Asakusa, Taitō-ku; ⏰7am-10pm, to 1am Wed & Thu, to 2am Fri & Sat; 🛜; 🚇Ginza line to Tawaramachi, exit 3)

'Cuzn Homeground
BAR

16 🚇 MAP P162, B1

Run by a wild gang of local hippies, 'Cuzn is the kind of bar where anything can happen: a barbecue, a jam session or all-night karaoke, for example. (カズンホームグラウンド; 📞03-5246-4380; www.homeground.jpn.com; 2-17-9 Asakusa, Taitō-ku; beer ¥900; ⏰noon-5am; 🛜; 🚇Ginza line to Tawaramachi, exit 3)

Kamiya Bar
BAR

17 🚇 MAP P162, C3

Kamiya opened in 1880 and is still hugely popular. The house drink for over a century is Denki Bran, a secret mix of brandy, gin, wine, curaçao and medicinal herbs. Order either 30 proof 'blanc' or 40 proof 'old' at the counter, then give your tickets to the server. (神谷バー; 📞03-3841-5400; www.kamiya-bar.com; 1-1-1 Asakusa, Taitō-ku; ⏰11.30am-10pm Wed-Mon; 🚇Ginza line to Asakusa, exit 3)

Entertainment

Oiwake
IZAKAYA

18 ⭐ MAP P162, A1

One of Tokyo's few minyō izakaya, where traditional folk music is performed, Oiwake is a homey place, where the waitstaff and the musicians are one and the same. Sets start at 7pm and 9pm; children are welcome for the early show. Tatami seating. (追分; 📞03-3844-6283; www.oiwake.info; 3-28-11 Nishi-Asakusa, Taitō-ku; ¥2000 plus 1 food item & 1 drink; ⏰5.30pm-midnight Tue-Sun; 🚇Tsukuba Express to Asakusa, exit 1)

Kappabashi-dōri

Kappabashi-dōri (合羽橋通り; Map p162, A2; www.kappabashi.or.jp; ⊙most shops 10am-5pm Mon-Sat; S Ginza line to Tawaramachi, exit 3) is the country's largest wholesale restaurant-supply and kitchenware district. Gourmet accessories include bamboo steamer baskets, lacquer trays, neon signs and *chōchin* (paper lanterns). It's also where restaurants get their freakishly realistic plastic food models.

Ganso Shokuhin Sample-ya (元祖食品サンプル屋; Map p162, A2; www.ganso-sample.com; 3-7-6 Nishi-Asakusa; ⊙10am-5.30pm) has a showroom of tongue-in-cheek ones, plus key chains and kits to make your own.

Staff at **Kama-asa** (Map p162, A2; ✆03-3841-9355; www.kama-asa.co.jp; 2-24-1 Matsugaya; ⊙10am-5.30pm) can advise you on the best locally made knife from their excellent selection. Also drop by **Soi** (Map p162, A1; ✆03-6802-7732; www.soi-2.jp; 3-25-11 Nishi-Asakusa; ⊙11am-6pm Tue-Sun) for a selection of ceramics and glassware, new and vintage, plus some cute *tenugui* (hand-dyed thin cotton towels) to wrap them in.

Shopping

Marugoto Nippon   FOOD & DRINKS

19 MAP P162, B2

Think of this as a mini mall, showcasing the best of Japan's speciality food and drink (ground floor) and arts and crafts (2nd floor). The 3rd floor showcases the products and attractions of different regions from around the country on a regularly changing basis. (まるごとにっぽん; ✆03-3845-0510; www.marugotonippon.com; 2-6-7 Asakusa, Taitō-ku; ⊙10am-8pm; S Ginza line to Tawaramachi, exit 3)

Bengara   ARTS & CRAFTS

20 MAP P162, C3

Noren are the curtains that hang in front of shop doors. This store sells beautiful ones, made of linen and coloured with natural dyes or decorated with ink-brush paintings. There are smaller items too, such as pouches and book covers, made of traditional textiles. (べんがら; ✆03-3841-6613; www.bengara.com; 1-35-6 Asakusa, Taitō-ku; ⊙10am-6pm Mon-Fri, to 7pm Sat & Sun, closed 3rd Thu of each month; S Ginza line to Asakusa, exit 1)

Fujiya   ARTS & CRAFTS

21 MAP P162, C2

Fujiya specialises in *tenugui*: dyed cloths of thin cotton that can be used as tea towels, handkerchiefs, gift wrapping (the list goes on – they're surprisingly versatile). Here they come in traditional designs and humorous modern ones. (ふじ屋; ✆03-3841-2283; 2-2-15 Asakusa, Taitō-ku; ⊙10am-6pm Thu-Tue; S Ginza line to Asakusa, exit 1)

Walking Tour 🥾

Kiyosumi-Shirakawa & Fukagawa

These peaceful residential areas east of the Sumida-gawa have become a base for small galleries, cool cafes and artisan businesses to set up shop. Spend a pleasant day away from the bustle of central Tokyo as you sip lattes, stroll around a traditional garden, ponder contemporary art and witness a spectacular fire ritual at a Buddhist temple.

Walk Facts

Start Iki Espresso;
Ⓢ Kiyosumi-Shirakawa
Station, exit A1

End Fukagawa Fudō-dō;
Ⓢ Monzen-Nakachō
Station, exit 1

Length 1.5km; two to three hours

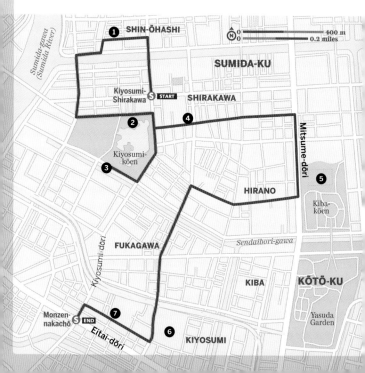

❶ Iki Espresso

Start the day at this Aussie-style **cafe** (☎03-6659-4654; www.iki espresso.com; 2-2-12 Tokiwa, Kōtō-ku; mains ¥1200-1350; ⏰8am-7pm; 📶) with a great breakfast of eggs, avocado on toast or a muffin, with coffee or fresh juice.

❷ Kiyosumi-teien

This picturesque **garden** (清澄庭園; ☎03-3641-5892; http://teien.tokyo-park.or.jp/en/kiyosumi; 3-3-9 Kiyosumi, Kōtō-ku; adult/child ¥150/free; ⏰9am-5pm) dates back to 1721. In the early 20th century Iwasaki Yatarō, founder of the Mitsubishi Corporation, purchased the property and added prize stones from across Japan around the pond.

❸ Babaghuri

Renewable, natural or recycled materials are used for the rustically beautiful clothes, pottery, tableware and linens sold in this **boutique** (☎03-3820-8825; www.babaghuri.jp; 3-1-7 Kiyosumi, Kōtō-ku; ⏰11am-7pm, irregular holidays).

❹ Fukagawa Edo Museum

See what this area looked liked during the Edo period (1603–1868) at this small **museum** (深川江戸資料館; ☎03-3630-8625; www.kcf.or.jp/fukagawa; 1-3-28 Shirakawa, Kōtō-ku; adult/child ¥400/50; ⏰9.30am-5pm, closed 2nd & 4th Mon of month).

❺ Museum of Contemporary Art, Tokyo (MOT)

This is Tokyo's premier contemporary arts **museum** (東京都現代美術館; ☎03-5245-4111; www.mot-art-museum.jp; 4-1-1 Miyoshi, Kōtō-ku; adult/child ¥500/free; ⏰10am-6pm Tue-Sun). The exhibitions cover all the major movements of post-WWII Japanese art, and include temporary shows on fashion, architecture and design.

❻ Tomioka Hachiman-gū

This attractive **shrine** (富岡八幡宮; ☎03-3642-1315; 1-20-3 Tomioka, Kōtō-ku) is famous as the birthplace of the sumo tournament. Around the back of the main building is the *yokozuna* (sumo grand champions) stone, carved with the names of each of these champion wrestlers.

❼ Fukagawa Fudō-dō

End by attending the 5pm *goma* (fire ritual) at **Fukagawa Fudō-dō** (深川不動尊; ☎03-3630-7020; www.fukagawafudou.gr.jp; 1-17-13 Tomioka, Kōtō-ku; ⏰8am-6pm, to 8pm on festival days). Sutras are chanted, giant *taiko* drums are pounded and flames are raised on the main altar as an offering to the deity. Also here is a trippy prayer corridor with 9500 miniature Fudōmyō (a fierce-looking representation of Buddha's determination) crystal statues.

Survival Guide

Tokyo Station (p41) SEAN PAVONE / SHUTTERSTOCK ©

Before You Go

Book Your Stay

Tokyo is known for being expensive; however, more attractive budget and midrange options are popping up every year. Levels of cleanliness and service are generally high everywhere.

'Business hotels' are functional midrange options that exist in every major hub.

Advance booking is highly recommended. You'll get a better price at most hotels, and even at hostels walk-ins can fluster staff .

Useful Websites

Jalan (www.jalan.net) Popular local discount accommodation site.

Japanese Inn Group (www.japanese inngroup.com) Bookings for ryokan and other small, family-run inns.

Lonely Planet (lonely planet.com/Japan/ Tokyo/hotels) Reviews and recommendations.

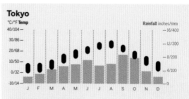

When to Go

Winter (Dec–Feb)
Cold but clear. December is lively with end-of-year celebrations; the city shuts down for the New Year holiday (1–3 Jan).

Spring (Mar–May)
Gradually warmer days; glorious cherry blossoms from late March to early April.

Summer (Jun–Aug)
Rainy season from June to mid-July, then hot and humid. City gets sleepy during the week-long O-Bon holiday in mid-August.

Autumn (Sep–Nov)
Warm days turn crisp and cool, with the odd typhoon in September and gorgeous autumn leaves in November.

Best Budget

Citan (☏ 03-6661-7559; https://backpackers japan.co.jp/citan; 15-2 Nihombashi-Odenmachō, Chūō-ku; dm/tw/d from ¥3000/8400/8500; ❄ 🛜 ; Ⓢ Shinjuku line to Bakuro-Yokoyama, exit A1) Flashpacker style without the price upgrade.

Mustard Hotel (マスタードホテル; ☏ 03-6459-2842; www.mustardhotel. com; 1-29 Higashi, Shibuya-ku; dm/s/d with shared bathroom from ¥4000/10,000/15,000,

s/d with bathroom from ¥20,000/25,000; 🍴 ❄ 🛜 ; 🚃 JR Yamanote line to Shibuya, new south exit) This design hostel in Shibuya also has budget-traveller-friendly dorms.

Bay Hotel Ginza (☏ 03-6226-1078; www. bay-hotel.jp/ginza; 7-13-15 Ginza, Chūō-ku; capsule ¥3500; 🍴 ❄ 🛜 ; Ⓢ Asakusa or Hibiya line to Higashi-Ginza, exit A3) Great value at this capsule hotel in a typically pricey neighbourhood.

Best Midrange

Apartment Hotel Mimaru Akasaka
(03-6807-4344; www.mimaruhotels.com; 7-9-6 Akasaka, Minato-ku; apt from ¥18,000; ❄ 🛜; ⑤ Chiyoda line to Akasaka, exit 7) Studio apartments priced nearly as low as a business hotel room.

Wired Hotel Asakusa
(03-5830-7931; www.wiredhotel.com; 2-16-2 Asakusa, Taitō-ku; tw/d from ¥13,000/14,000; 🍽 ❄ 🛜; ⑤ Ginza line to Asakusa, exit 1) Good-value design hotel, near the sights in Asakusa.

Hotel Niwa Tokyo (庭のホテル; 03-3293-0028; www.hotelniwatokyo.com; 1-1-6 Misaki-chō, Chiyoda-ku; s/d/tw from ¥14,600/17,200/20,600; ❄ @ 🛜; 🚆 JR Sōbu line to Suidōbashi, east exit) Traditional design flourishes at this better-than-ordinary hotel in centrally located Suidōbashi.

Best Top End

Park Hyatt Tokyo
(パークハイアット東京; 03-5322-1234; http://tokyo.park.hyatt.com; 3-7-1-2 Nishi-Shinjuku, Shinjuku-ku; d from ¥60,000; ❄ @ 🛜 🏊; ⑤ Ōedo

line to Tochōmae, exit A4) Palatial high-rise atop a Shinjuku skyscraper.

Hilltop Hotel (山の上ホテル; 03-3293-2311; www.yamanoue-hotel.co.jp; 1-1 Kanda-Surugadai, Chiyoda-ku; s/d from ¥22,575/33,265; ❄ @ 🛜; 🚆 JR Chūō or Sōbu lines to Ochanomizu, Ochanomizu exit) Art deco style and literary cred (and not really all that expensive).

Aman Tokyo (03-5224-3333; www.aman.com; 1-5-6 Ōtemachi, Chiyoda-ku; r from ¥120,000; ❄ @ 🛜 🏊; ⑤ Marunouchi line to Ōtemachi, exit A5) Go big or go home: this is the ultimate Tokyo splurge.

Best Ryokan

Sawanoya Ryokan
(旅館澤の屋; 03-3822-2251; www.sawanoya.com; 2-3-11 Yanaka, Taitō-ku; s/d from ¥5615/10,585; 🍽 ❄ @ 🛜; ⑤ Chiyoda line to Nezu, exit 1) Hits all the right notes, from the thoughtful service to the relaxing traditional baths.

Hoshinoya Tokyo
(星のや東京; 050-3786-1144; www.hoshinoyatokyo.com; 1-9-1 Ōtemachi, Chiyoda-ku;

r incl breakfast from ¥166,000; ⑤ Marunouchi line to Ōtemachi, exit A1) The ultimate luxury ryokan experience.

Kimi Ryokan (貴美旅館; 03-3971-3766; www.kimi-ryokan.jp; 2-36-8 Ikebukuro, Toshima-ku; s/d from ¥5400/8100; 🍽 ❄ @ 🛜; 🚆 JR Yamanote line to Ikebukuro, west exit) The gracious hospitality of a high-end ryokan, without the price tag.

Arriving in Tokyo

Narita Airport

Narita Airport (成田空港; NRT; 0476-34-8000; www.narita-airport.jp; 🛜), 66km east of Tokyo, has three terminals, with Terminal 3 handling low-cost carriers. All terminals have tourist information desks.

Haneda Airport

Closer to central Tokyo, **Haneda Airport** (羽田空港; HND; international terminal 03-6428-0888; www.haneda-airport.jp; 🛜) has two domestic terminals and one international terminal. Note that some international flights arrive at awkward night-time hours, between midnight and 5am, when the only public transport to central Tokyo will be infrequent night buses and taxis.

Tokyo Station

Tokyo Station (東京駅; Map p40; www.tokyostation city.com; 1-9 Marunouchi, Chiyoda-ku; 🚆 JR lines to Tokyo Station) is the terminus for all *shinkansen*, the bullet trains that connect Tokyo to major cities all over Japan. From Tokyo Station you can transfer to the JR Chūō and JR Yamanote lines, as well as the Marunouchi subway line.

Getting Around

Bicycle

Tokyo is not a bicycle-friendly city. Despite this you'll see locals on bikes everywhere.
    Some accommodation has bikes

to lend, sometimes for free or for a small fee. For exploring the neighbourhoods of Ueno and Yanesen, check out **Tokyobike Rentals Yanaka** (Map p146; 📞03-5809-0980; www.tokyobikerentals.com; 4-2-39 Yanaka, Taitō-ku; 1st day ¥3000, additional day ¥1500; ⏰10am-7.30pm Wed-Mon; 🚆JR Yamanote line to Nippori, west exit). In Yurakuchō, **Muji** (無印良品; Map p40; 📞03-5208-8241; www.muji.com/jp/flagship/yurakucho/en; 3-8-3 Marunouchi, Chiyoda-ku; ⏰10am-9pm; 🚆JR Yamanote line to Yūrakuchō, Kyōbashi exit) has bikes to rent (¥1080 per day; from 10am to 8pm; passport required).

Boat

Two operators – **Tokyo Cruise** (水上バス; Map p162, C3) Suijō Bus; 📞0120-977-311; http://suijobus.co.jp) and **Tokyo Mizube Cruising Line** (東京水辺ライン; 📞03-5608-8869; www.tokyo-park.or.jp/waterbus) – run water buses up and down the Sumida-gawa (Sumida River). Tickets can be purchased subject to availability before departure at any pier.

Bus

Toei (www.kotsu.metro.tokyo.jp/eng/services/bus.html) runs an extensive bus network, though it's rarely more convenient than the subway.

Taxi

⊙ Fares start at ¥410 for the first 1km, then rise by ¥80 for every 237m you travel or for every 90 seconds spent in traffic.

⊙ There's a surcharge of 20% between 10pm and 5am.

⊙ Drivers rarely speak English, though fortunately most taxis have navigation systems. It's a good idea to have your destination written down in Japanese, or better yet, a business card with an address.

⊙ Taxis take credit cards and IC passes.

⊙ Tokyo strictly regulates ride-sharing apps: only licensed chauffeurs can offer rides, meaning you're more likely to summon a town car that costs more than a regular taxi.

Train & Subway

Tokyo's extensive rail network includes JR

Tickets & Passes

Prepaid, rechargeable Suica and Pasmo cards (they're interchangeable) work on all city trains, subways and buses. Purchase from any touch-screen ticket-vending machine (including those at Haneda and Narita airports); most have an English option. JR stations sell Suica; subway and independent lines sell Pasmo. Both require a ¥500 deposit, which is refunded (along with any remaining charge) when you return the pass to any ticket window.

Passes can be topped-up at any touch-screen ticket-vending machine (not just, for example, at JR stations for Suica passes) in increments of ¥1000. To use the cards, just run them over the card readers at the ticket gates upon entering and exiting. If you somehow manage to invalidate your card, take it to the station window and staff will sort it out. Fares for pass users are slightly less (a few yen per journey) than for paper-ticket holders.

lines, a subway system and private commuter lines that depart in every direction for the suburbs, like spokes on a wheel. Journeys that require transfers between lines run by different operators cost more than journeys that use only one operator's lines. Major transit hubs include Tokyo, Shinagawa, Shibuya, Shinjuku, Ikebukuro and Ueno stations. Trains arrive and depart precisely on time and are generally clean and pleasant, though they get uncomfortably crowded during rush hours.

Tickets

o Single-ride paper tickets can be purchased at touch-screen ticket-vending machines outside station ticket gates.

o To purchase the correct ticket, you'll need to work out the fare from the chart above the machines. If you're unsure, just buy a ticket for the cheapest fare (you can sort it out when you exit).

o Insert your ticket in the slot at the gate (only some of the ticket gates will have slots for paper tickets). Make sure to pick it up when it pops out again.

o You'll do the same thing when you exit. If your ticket does not have sufficient charge to cover your journey, insert it into one of the 'fare adjustment' machines near the exit gates.

Essential Information

Accessible Travel

Tokyo is making steps to improve universal access – or *bariafurī* (barrier free; バリアフリー) in Japanese. It is a slow process, though one that has gotten a boost from the 2021 Olympics preparations.

Accessible Japan

(www.accessible-japan.com) is the best resource; they also produce an ebook with lots of detail.

Download Lonely Planet's free *Accessible Travel* guide from https://shop.lonelyplanet.com/categories/accessible-travel.com.

Business Hours

Note that some outdoor attractions (such as gardens) may close earlier in the winter. Standard opening hours:

Banks 9am to 3pm (some to 5pm) Monday to Friday

Bars 6pm to late, with no fixed closing hours

Boutiques noon to 8pm, irregularly closed

Cafes vary enormously; chains 7am to 10pm

Department stores 10am to 8pm

Museums 9am or 10am to 5pm; often closed Monday

Post offices 9am to 5pm Monday to Friday

Restaurants lunch 11.30am to 2pm, dinner 6pm to 10pm; last orders taken about half an hour before closing

Discount Cards

Grutto Pass (¥2200; www.rekibun.or.jp/grutto) offers free or discounted admission to 90+ Tokyo attractions (mostly museums). This usually pays for itself after a few museum visits. All participating venues sell them.

Electricity

Type A
100V/50Hz

Emergency

Ambulance & Fire ☏119

Police ☏110

Police Consultation Hotline ☏03-3501-0110 (24 hours; translation services available

8.30am to 5.15pm Monday to Friday)

Japan Helpline (☏0570-000-911; 24 hours) All purpose, English-language information hotline; for data users, contact them via the web form online at jhelp.com.

Tokyo Medical Info Hotline (☏03-5285-8181 (9am to 8pm)

Internet

Decent wi-fi is standard in Tokyo accommodation (though exceptions exist). The city has an increasing number of free hotspots, which can be found on subway platforms, on the streets of some districts and at many convenience stores, major attractions and shopping centres. Look for the sticker that says 'Japan Wi-Fi'.

Money

ATMs

Most Japanese bank ATMs do not accept foreign-issued cards. Even if they display Visa and MasterCard logos, most accept only Japan-issued versions of these cards.

Money-Saving Tips

o Many of Tokyo's more expensive restaurants are comparatively reasonable at lunch; you'll get better value if you splurge at midday.

o After 5pm, grocery stores, bakeries and even department store food halls slash prices on *bentō* (boxed meals), baked goods and sushi.

o Check out **Tokyo Cheapo** (http://tokyo cheapo.com) for other money-saving tips.

Seven Bank ATMs at 7-Eleven convenience stores and Japan Post Bank ATMs at post offices accept most overseas cards and have instructions in English. Seven Bank ATMs are accessible 24 hours a day.

There is a withdrawal limit of ¥100,000 per transaction at Seven Bank ATMs (and ¥50,000 at Japan Post Bank ATMs). Bear in mind that your bank or card company may impose an even stricter limit; if your card is rejected, this might be the reason why.

Credit Cards

Most businesses in Tokyo now accept credit cards, usually displaying the logo for the cards they accept on the cash register.

Some cheaper cafes only accept cash, so it may be helpful to carry some cash. If in doubt, ask upfront.

Visa is the most widely accepted, followed by MasterCard, American Express and Diners Club. Foreign-issued cards should work fine. The standard in Japan is a chip card that requires a PIN for verification.

Public Holidays

If a national holiday falls on a Monday, most museums and restaurants that normally close on Mondays will remain open and close the next day instead.

New Year's Day (Ganjitsu) 1 January

Coming-of-Age Day (Seijin-no-hi) Second Monday in January

National Foundation Day (Kenkoku Kinen-bi) 11 February

Emperor's Birthday (Tennō-no-Tanjōbi) 23 February

Spring Equinox (Shumbun-no-hi) 20 or 21 March

Shōwa Day (Shōwa-no-hi) 29 April

Constitution Day (Kempō Kinem-bi) 3 May

Green Day (Midori-no-hi) 4 May

Children's Day (Kodomo-no-hi) 5 May

Marine Day (Umi-no-hi) Third Monday in July

Mountain Day (Yama-no-hi) 11 August

Respect-for-the-Aged Day (Keirō-no-hi) Third Monday in September

Autumn Equinox (Shūbun-no-hi) 23 or 24 September

Health & Sports Day (Taiiku-no-hi) Second Monday in October

Culture Day (Bunka-no-hi) 3 November

Labour Thanksgiving Day (Kinrō Kansha-no-hi) 23 November

Safe Travel

The biggest threat to travellers in Tokyo is the city's general aura of safety; keep up the same level of caution and common sense that you would back home.

○ Drink-spiking continues to be a problem in Roppongi (resulting in robbery, extortion and, in extreme cases, physical assault). This is most often the case when touts are involved; never follow a tout into a bar, anywhere.

○ Men are likely to be solicited in Roppongi and neighbourhoods that are considered red-light districts, including Kabukichō (in Shinjuku) and Dōgenzaka (in Shibuya). Women – particularly solo women –

are likely to be harassed in these districts.

○ Groping does sometimes occur on crowded trains. Most Tokyo train lines have women-only carriages at peak times. These are marked with signs (usually pink) in Japanese and English. Children can ride in them, too.

○ COVID-19 cases and casualties in Tokyo were low compared to many cities abroad; however, Japan's slow vaccine rollout has meant prolonged community transmission and a heightened chance for new variants to emerge. Travellers are advised to check the latest

information before making travel plans; current border restrictions and quarantine protocols are posted on the Ministry of Foreign Affairs website (www.mofa.go.jp).

Telephone

Country code ☏81

International access code ☏001

Tokyo area code ☏03

Mobile Phones

Japan operates on the 3G network, so compatible phones should work in Tokyo. Prepaid data-only SIM cards for unlocked smartphones are widely available and can be purchased at kiosks in the arrival halls at both Narita and Haneda airports, and also from dedicated desks at major electronics retailers like Bic Camera and Yodobashi Camera.

Getting the SIM to work may require some fiddling with settings, so make sure you've got a connection before you leave the counter. Staff usually speak some English.

Currently only **Mobal** (www.mobal. com) offers SIMs that

Dos & Don'ts

○ Relax. Japan is known for its hair-splitting etiquette rules, but foreign tourists are given a pass for just about everything.

○ Pack light. Tokyo hotel rooms are small, with little room for luggage.

○ Dress smart if you want to blend in, although for all but the fanciest restaurants, casual clothes are fine.

○ Wear shoes you can slip on and off easily, as many ryokan and restaurants still ask you to leave your shoes at the door.

○ Refrain from eating on the subway or while walking down the street – it's considered impolite.

○ Get in line. The Japanese are famous queuers.

give you an actual phone number from which to make and receive calls; they offer English language support and can ship to your accommodation. Otherwise, the variety is huge, and which one to go with depends on the length of your stay and how much data you need.

Public Phones

Public phones, most commonly located around train stations, do still exist. Ordinary public phones are green; those that allow you to call abroad are grey and are usually marked 'International & Domestic Card/Coin Phone'.

Local calls cost ¥10 per minute; note that you won't get change on a ¥100 coin. The minimum charge for international calls is ¥100, which buys you a fraction of a minute. Dial 001 010 (KDDI), 0061 010 (SoftBank Telecom) or 0033 010 (NTT), followed by the country code, area code and local number. There's very little difference in the rates from the different providers; all offer better

rates at night. Reverse-charge (collect) international calls can be made by dialling 0051.

Toilets

o Tokyo has few actual public toilets; most people prefer the privately maintained ones provided by train stations, tourist attractions, department stores and malls, which tend to be nicer.

o Toilets are typically marked with generic gendered pictograms; but just in case, note the characters for female (女) and male (男). Newer or recently redeveloped buildings may have 'multifunctional' (多機能; takinō) restrooms; these large, separate rooms are wheelchair accessible, may have nappy changing or ostomate facilities, and are gender-neutral.

o Toilet paper is usually available, but it's still a good idea to have a packet of tissues on hand. Paper towels and hand dryers may or may not be present; most Japanese carry a handkerchief for use after washing their hands.

o Separate toilet slippers will be provided in establishments where you take off your shoes at the entrance; they are typically just inside the toilet door.

Tourist Information

Tokyo Metropolitan Government Building Tourist Information Center (☑ 03-5321-3077; info@tokyo-tourism.jp; 1st fl, Tokyo Metropolitan Government bldg 1, 2-8-1 Nishi-Shinjuku, Shinjuku-ku; ⊙ 9.30am-6.30pm; S Ōedo line to Tochōmae, exit A4) Has English-language information and publications. There are additional branches in Keisei Ueno Station, Haneda Airport and Shinjuku Bus Terminal.

JNTO Tourist Information Center (Map p40, C4; ☑ 03-3201-3331; www.jnto.go.jp; 1st fl, Shin-Tokyo Bldg, 3-3-1 Marunouchi, Chiyoda-ku; ⊙ 9am-5pm; ☎; S Chiyoda line to Nijūbashimae, exit 1) Run by the Japan National Tourism Organisation (JNTO), this TIC has information on Tokyo and beyond. Staff speak English.

JR East Travel Service Center (JR東日本トラベルサービスセンター; Map p40, D3; ☏03-5221-8123; www.jreast.co.jp; Tokyo Station, 1-9-1 Marunouchi, Chiyoda-ku; ⏱7.30am-8.30pm; 📶; 🚉JR Yamanote line to Tokyo, Marunouchi north exit) Tourist information, rail passes, money exchange, same-day baggage storage (¥600), porter services and bookings for ski and onsen getaways. Staff speak English.

Visas

Citizens of 68 countries/regions, including Australia, Canada, Hong Kong, Korea, New Zealand, Singapore, USA, UK and almost all European nations, will be automatically issued a temporary visitor visa on arrival. Typically this visa is good for 90 days.

For a complete list of visa-exempt countries and durations, consult www.mofa.go.jp.

Responsible Travel

Overtourism

Tokyo being huge, the city has so far largely been able to absorb the rising number of tourists. Locals are less likely to grumble if visitors abide by established etiquette norms, such as queuing and refraining from loud conversations (especially on public transportation).

One complaint that is common in the restaurant industry is no-shows; if you cannot make your reservation, please call (or have your accommodation call for you), otherwise the restaurant takes the loss on the ingredients purchased specifically for your party – and may hesitate to accept reservations from overseas guests in the future.

Support Local & Give Back

Find accommodation through **Japanese Guesthouses** (www.japaneseguesthouses.com), which lists small, family-run inns.

Leave a Light Footprint

○ Refuse packaging by saying, *'Fukuro wa irimasen'* (I don't need a bag), at the cash register, or just hold up a reusable shopping bag to show you've already got one.

○ Limit your consumption of seafood threatened by over-fishing, such as *unagi* (eel) and *maguro* (tuna) – including *toro* (fatty tuna belly).

○ Skip vending machines, which use up a considerable amount of energy.

○ Carry your own water bottle and find refilling stations with the app **mymizu** (www.mymizu.co).

Language

Japanese pronunciation is easy for English speakers, as most of its sounds are also found in English. Note though that it's important to make the distinction between short and long vowels, as vowel length can change the meaning of a word. The long vowels (**ā, ē, ī, ō, ū**) should be held twice as long as the short ones. All syllables in a word are pronounced fairly evenly in Japanese. If you read our pronunciation guides as if they were English, you'll be understood.

To enhance your trip with a phrasebook, visit **lonelyplanet.com**.

Basics

Hello.
こんにちは。　　　　*kon·ni·chi·wa*

Goodbye.
さようなら。　　　　*sa·yō·na·ra*

Yes.
はい。　　　　*hai*

No.
いいえ。　　　　*ī·e*

Please.
ください。　　　　*ku·da·sai*

Thank you.
ありがとう。　　　　*a·ri·ga·tō*

Excuse me.
すみません。　　　　*su·mi·ma·sen*

Sorry.
ごめんなさい。　　　　*go·men·na·sai*

What's your name?
お名前は
何ですか？　　　　*o·na·ma·e wa nan des ka*

My name is ...
私の
名前は…です。　　　　*wa·ta·shi no na·ma·e wa ...des*

Do you speak English?
英語が
話せますか？　　　　*ē·go ga ha·na·se·mas ka*

I don't understand.
わかりません。　　　　*wa·ka·ri·ma·sen*

Eating & Drinking

I'd like to reserve a table for (two).
（2人）の
予約を　お
願いします。　　　　*(fu·ta·ri) no yo·ya·ku o o·ne·gai shi·mas*

I'd like (the menu).
（メニュー）
をお願いします。　　　　*(me·nyū) o o·ne·gai shi·mas*

I don't eat (red meat).
（赤身の肉）
は食べません。　　　　*(a·ka·mi no ni·ku) wa ta·be·ma·sen*

That was delicious!
おいしかった。　　　　*oy·shi·kat·ta*

Please bring the bill.
お勘定
をください。　　　　*o·kan·jō o ku·da·sai*

Cheers!	乾杯!	*kam·pai*
beer	ビール	*bī·ru*
coffee	コーヒー	*kō·hī*

Shopping

I'd like ...
…をください。　　　　*... o ku·da·sai*

I'm just looking.
見ているだけです。　　　　*mi·te·i·ru da·ke des*

How much is it?
いくらですか？ *i·ku·ra des ka*

That's too expensive.
高すぎます。 *ta·ka·su·gi·mas*

Can you give me a discount?
ディスカウント *dis·kown·to*
できますか？ *de·ki·mas ka*

Emergencies

Help!
たすけて！ *tas·ke·te*

Go away!
離れろ！ *ha·na·re·ro*

Call the police!
警察を呼んで！ *kē·sa·tsu o yon·de*

Call a doctor!
医者を呼んで！ *i·sha o yon·de*

I'm lost.
迷いました。 *ma·yoy·mash·ta*

I'm ill.
私は病 *wa·ta·shi wa*
気です。 *byō·ki des*

Where are the toilets?
トイレは *toy·re wa*
どこですか？ *do·ko des ka*

Time & Numbers

What time is it?
何時ですか？ *nan·ji des ka*

It's (10) o'clock.
(10)時です。 *(jū)·ji des*

Half past (10).
(10)時半です。 *(jū)·ji han des*

morning	朝	*a·sa*
afternoon	午後	*go·go*
evening	夕方	*yū·ga·ta*

yesterday	きのう	*ki·nō*
today	今日	*kyō*
tomorrow	明日	*a·shi·ta*

1	一	*i·chi*
2	二	*ni*
3	三	*san*
4	四	*shi/yon*
5	五	*go*
6	六	*ro·ku*
7	七	*shi·chi/ na·na*
8	八	*ha·chi*
9	九	*ku/kyū*
10	十	*jū*

Transport & Directions

Where's the ...?
…はどこ *... wa do·ko*
ですか？ *des ka*

What's the address?
住所は何 *jū·sho wa nan*
ですか？ *des ka*

Can you show me (on the map)?
(地図で)教えて *(chi·zu de)*
o·shi·e·te
くれませんか？ *ku·re·ma·sen ka*

When's the next (bus)?
次の(バス)は *tsu·gi no (bas) wa*
何時ですか？ *nan·ji des ka*

Does it stop at ...?
…に *... ni*
停まりますか？ *to·ma·ri·mas ka*

Please tell me when we get to ...
… に着いたら *... ni tsu·i·ta·ra*
教えてください。 *o·shi·e·te ku·da·sai*

Behind the Scenes

Send Us Your Feedback

We love to hear from travellers – your comments help make our books better. We read every word, and we guarantee that your feedback goes straight to the authors. Visit **lonelyplanet.com/contact** to submit your updates and suggestions.

Note: We may edit, reproduce and incorporate your comments in Lonely Planet products such as guidebooks, websites and digital products, so let us know if you don't want your comments reproduced or your name acknowledged. For a copy of our privacy policy visit lonelyplanet.com/privacy.

Simon's Thanks

Many thanks to co-writer Rebecca and to the following: Will Andrews, Toshiko Ishii, Kenichi, Giles Murray, Chris Kirkland, Shoji Kobayashi, Jun Onuma, Sabrina Suljevic, Ken Gail Kato, Toyokuni Honda, Tim Hornyak and Tomoko Yoshizawa.

Rebecca's Thanks

Thank you to my family and friends, who are there for me through all the ups and downs and late nights; to my indefatigable co-author Simon, for his inspiration and guidance; to LP for standing by me; and to all the chefs, curators, professors, baristas and total strangers who knowingly or unknowingly provided me with new insight into this city, which I must also thank, for always keeping me on my toes.

Acknowledgements

Cover photographs: (front) Tokyo street, VTT Studio/Shutterstock ©; (back) Cherry blossoms in Naka-Meguro, Sakarin Sawasdinaka/Shutterstock ©

This Book

This 8th edition of Lonely Planet's *Pocket Tokyo* guidebook was researched and written by Simon Richmond and Rebecca Milner, who also wrote the previous two editions. This guidebook was produced by the following:

Destination Editors Laura Crawford, James Smart

Senior Product Editors Kate Chapman, Sandie Kestell

Regional Senior Cartographer Diana Von Holdt

Product Editors Carolyn Boicos, Jessica Ryan

Book Designers Norma Prause-Brewer, Wibowo Rusli

Assisting Editors Janet Austin, Janice Bird, Lauren O'Connell, Kristin Odijk

Assisting Cartographers Michael Garrett, Corey Hutchison

Cover Researcher Brendan Dempsey-Spencer

Thanks to Naoko Akamatsu, Hannah Cartmel, Gwen Cotter, Sasha Drew, Bruce Evans, Victoria Harrison, Karen Henderson, Graham Holey, Andi Jones, Sonia Kapoor, Darren O'Connell, Genna Patterson, Claire Rourke

Index

See also separate subindexes for:

- ⊗ **Eating p189**
- 🍷 **Drinking p190**
- 🎭 **Entertainment p190**
- 🛍 **Shopping p190**

Sights 000
Map Pages **000**

Our

journalist and photographer Simon Richmond has specialised as a travel writer since the early 1990s, and first worked for Lonely Planet in 1999 on its *Central Asia* guide. He's long since stopped counting the number of guidebooks he's researched and written for Lonely Planet, but countries covered include Australia, China, India, Iran, Japan, Korea, Malaysia, Mongolia, Myanmar (Burma), Russia, Singapore, South Africa and Turkey. For Lonely Planet's website he's penned features on topics from the world's best swimming pools to the joys of urban sketching – follow him on Instagram to see some of his photos and sketches.

Rebecca Milner

California-born Rebecca has been living in Tokyo since 2002. She is the co-writer of Lonely Planet guides to Tokyo and Japan, and is a freelance writer covering travel, food and culture. Her work has been published in the *Guardian,* the *Independent,* the *Sunday Times Travel Magazine,* the *Japan Times* and more.

Published by Lonely Planet Global Limited
CRN 554153
8th edition – Feb 2022
ISBN 978 1 78868 380 7
© Lonely Planet 2022 Photographs © as indicated 2022
10 9 8 7 6 5 4 3 2 1
Printed in Singapore